Narrative Techniques and their Effects in

"La Mort le Roi Artu"

Narrative Techniques and their Effects in

"La Mort le Roi Artu"

by

Atie Dingemans Zuurdeeg

French Literature Publications Company
York, South Carolina
1981

**To the memory of
my husband and parents**

PREFACE

For the method used in the following monograph I am greatly indebted to Professor Eugène Vinaver who in his works and lectures has pointed out the various narrative techniques used in the composition of Medieval romances. The purpose of this study is to determine to what extent and to what effect the author of *La Mort le Roi Artu* has made use of these devices.

Since *La Mort* forms an integral part of the voluminous *Vulgate Cycle,* critics have given particular attention to the many themes which link this final romance to preceding parts of the *Cycle.* For this reason I have concentrated on the cohesive elements within the romance. While reference to previous events was often necessary for clarification or a fuller understanding, the focus of my analysis is the manner in which the author has arranged the material so that it can be read as a romance in its own right.

I want to thank Augustana College for partially funding this publication.

CONTENTS

INTRODUCTION

The thirteenth century romance *La Mort le Roi Artu* forms the last part of the prose *Lancelot* which in turn concludes the *Vulgate Cycle*. *La Mort le Roi Artu* follows *La Queste del Saint Graal* and describes the death of King Arthur, the destruction of his realm, and the dissolution of the fellowship of the Round Table.

The only existing complete edition of the whole cycle of romances is that of Oskar H. Sommer.[1] Of this series volume 6, which appeared in 1913, contains both "Les Aventures ou La Queste del Saint Graal" and "La Mort le Roi Artu." Several scholars, however, have published parts of the cycle in separate editions. There are two such editions of the final romance, *La Mort le Roi Artu,* one by J. Douglas Bruce,[2] and a more recent one by Jean Frappier.[3]

Two critics who concern themselves with the cycle as a whole or a considerable part of it, are Ferdinand Lot[4] and J. Douglas Bruce.[5] Both are primarily interested in sources and authorship. Lot argues for the unity of the cycle. He points to the pattern of *entrelacement* which links the different parts, to demonstrate that the cycle must be the work of one author. Bruce, on the other hand, believes in a number of authors, because he finds that the various parts are written in different styles.

Bruce not only compares the different styles, he also evaluates them. In *La Mort le Roi Artu* he deplores, for instance, the inclusion of the story of the lady of Beloé as an "inopportune invention of the author." But he approves "the minimum of digressions," and he praises the author because he "does not aim at engaging or holding the reader's attention by cheap supernaturalism or by the puerile extravagance of his hero's exploits or by appeals to the prevalent taste for the artificial fashions ⌐f courtly love."[6]   In fact, Bruce approves precisely those aspects of the romance which, he believes, deviate from the typical medieval patterns.   But such approval seems misplaced, for it rests on a set of classical criteria, such as unity and concentration, which are inappropriate to a medieval composition.

Only two critics, Marjorie B. Fox and Jean Frappier, have offered analyses of the entire *Mort le Roi Artu,* although several articles have considered specific aspects of it.[7]   Fox's principal concern is source study.   In the first part of her book, *La Mort le Roi Artus,*[8] she traces the origin of the various episodes and characters; in the second part she analyzes the composition of the romance in terms of how the author has used the material at his disposal.   She concludes that the author was more interested in the arrangement of the episodes than in the preservation of the characters of the protagonists.   This observation is significant for the present study.

Jean Frappier's *Etude sur La Mort le Roi Artu,*[9] which appeared three years after *La Mort le Roi Artus,* deals with the "spirit" and form of the romance, as well as with sources and authorship.   Frappier disagrees with Lot and shares the opinion of Bruce and Albert Pauphilet[10] that different authors wrote the various romances which make up the *Lancelot-Graal* cycle. But while the latter deny any unity to the cyclic composition, Frappier argues for an "architect" who provided the general outline, to account for the many themes which connect the different parts.   Of particular interest for this monograph is Frappier's interpretation of the romance.   Since structure and meaning form the subject of the following pages, a brief discussion of the principal points of Frappier's study seems appropriate.

In Frappier's view the characters are drawn with psychological realism.   He praises the author for breaking with stylized abstractions and giving us instead "realistic portraits of individuals."   Consequently, Frappier's analysis of the romance centers around the characters of the individual heroes.   In the introduction to his edition of *La Mort le Roi Artu* he writes: "L'action progresse surtout par les passions des personnages; les fatalités intérieures de l'amour et de la haine déclenchent et soutiennent le crescendo de la mort à travers tout le roman."[11] Since the emotions of the individual heroes determine the action, other forces can only be effective to the extent that the characters allow themselves to be controlled by them. One such force is destiny. While admitting that destiny is the dominant theme of the romance, Frappier does not see it as a destructive force which operates independently: "Seule l'erreur humaine permet au Destin d'exercer son impitoyable rigueur. . . .le romancier de *La Mort Artu* a situé strictement le problème du Destin sur le plan le plus humain, celui de la vie intérieure."[12]

For the psychological point of view it is necessary that the characters of the protagonists remain consistent throughout the cycle of romances. The position of *La Mort le Roi Artu* as a sequel to the *Queste* presents a problem here because of the obvious difference in spirit between the two romances. In the *Queste* religion is the dominant theme and the heroes' conduct is judged by Christian standards. In its sequel however, very few references are made to religion and the norms which govern the heroes' behavior appear to be of an entirely worldly nature. In Frappier's words: "On ne trouve plus dans la dernière partie du *Lancelot en prose* l'inspiration cistercienne de l'avant-dernière partie" and "la grande flamme mystique de la *Queste* s'est presque éteinte dans *La Mort Artu*."[13] Frappier then solves this problem of incongruity as follows: "La grande originalité du romancier de *La Mort Artu* est ici de placer la conquête du Graal dans l'âme de l'homme. Le Graal est intérieur, et les aventures qui conduisent à lui sont des aventures psychologiques."[14] As an example of the effect of religion on the individual characters he cites Lancelot: "Au début de *La Mort Artu*, Lancelot vit de nouveau dans le péché; à la fin il est au bord de la sainteté. On peut dire qu'il remplit dans le roman tout l'intervalle entre les deux états."[15]

Both destiny and religion are thus internalized. But, if both forces are at work in the individual, which one is actually in command? How can God and Fate be reconciled? To this question Frappier responds that the concept of destiny in the romance lies halfway between the pagan concept in which Fate was an independent force and the Christian concept in which Fate is subordinated to God. In the romance God and F each rule their own domain: "La Roue de Fortune est de la fatalité qui détruit les puissances de chair san. vienne la notion de mérite ou de démérite. Mais n'appartiennent qu'à Dieu. . ."[16] Accordingly Fate would be responsible for the love between Lancelot and Guinevere, but God for dissolving it and elevating it to the level of divine love. Thus Frappier acknowledges the prominent roles of both God and Fate in this romance, but subordinates them to the character of the individual hero whose decisions trigger action and reaction and determine the course of events and its outcome.

Even though Frappier's impressive study is still considered authoritative, this interpretation of the romance in terms of psychological realism leaves room for other points of view. The present monograph is an attempt to analyze the romance from the perspective of its narrative techniques. It is not concerned with authorship or origins, neither does it presume to cover all aspects and every detail of the narrative. Its purpose is to arrive at an interpretation of the principal themes, episodes, and characters by means of an analysis of the structure of the romance.

In several respects the meaning thus discovered will differ from Frappier's conclusions. For instance, destiny is seen as an independent force which controls the action whether the characters cooperate or not. Religion, on the other hand, does not appear to play a role in the main body of the narrative, and, while Frappier states that the psychology of the individual is enveloped by that of the group, the structural approach leads to the opposite conclusion. Although the characters are presented with life and vigor and not as stylized abstractions, still their actions are determined by a set of ideologies prevalent in Medieval French literature. They are not, that is, fully independent creations. Their behavior is prescribed by the codes of chivalry, courtly love, and family honor. The following chapters will show that ideological rather than psychological conflicts form the basis of the events which take place in *La Mort le Roi Artu.*

I

FATE AND SUSPENSE:
two downward Movements

The opening paragraph of *La Mort le Roi Artu* serves as an introduction to both the author and the romance. The author presents himself as Gautier Map. At King Henry's request he has written a sequel to his previous romance, the *Aventures del Seint Graal*, to relate how those whose heroic deeds he told before came to their end. He explains the title by the final event, the battle of Salisbury Plain, in which King Arthur is mortally wounded. Thus, in a few lines, the author has situated the romance between two specific events, the quest of the Holy Grail and the defeat and death of King Arthur.

A downward movement is clearly indicated. It will be steep and powerful, for it transports the knights of the Round Table from the highest to the lowest point in the cycle of their adventures. In the quest a few of their number attained a spiritual summit when they were admitted into the presence of the Holy Grail. The others were judged unworthy of this honor. They will now go down to death and destruction. Even King Arthur, until now the invulnerable figurehead and symbol of knighthood, will be defeated in battle. So, at the very onset of new (non-) adventures, the author rings the death-knell over Arthur's realm. He dispels any hope of a favorable outcome, and communicates a sense of impending and inevitable doom.

The presentation of *La Mort le Roi Artu* as a sequel to the Grail adventures is much more than a simple linking-up of the two romances. As we will see, past events have cast their shadows far ahead and will come to bear on the future of the company of the Round Table.

The first indications of what that future will hold are somber indeed. As we learn from the knight Bohort, the fellowship of knights has recently been depleted by more than a fifth. Just returned from Jerusalem, Bohort has come to report to King Arthur on the adventures of the knights in their search for the Holy Grail. Galahad and Perceval are mourned, but all at court find comfort, we must assume, in the fact that they gave their lives to the highest cause. Many others, however, died less honorable deaths. When the king has recorded all the Grail adventures, he inquires how many knights have been lost. It appears that thirty-two are missing from their midst. So, contrary to the display of strength and confidence at the beginning of many earlier adventures, the opening scene here shows weakness and loss.

Weakness appears not only in loss of numbers, but more seriously, in unworthy conduct. Many knights were killed as a result of quarreling among themselves. The character of Gawain is a case in point. King Arthur, who has heard that Gawain is responsible for many deaths, summons him to explain. Gawain admits to having killed eighteen knights—among them King Baudemagus, a knight whom King Arthur valued highly. These killings were shameful, Gawain confesses, acts not of chivalry, but of *mescheance* and *pechié*. The meaning of these two words, especially of the former, is not immediately clear. Since they reappear many times in the narrative, they deserve a closer examination at this point.

When he speaks of his *grant mescheance* Gawain says: "la mescheance se torna plus vers moi que vers nul de mes compaignons" (3:21-23).[1] Apparently he refers to a force outside of him which drove him to these acts. In saying that fortune turned against him Gawain seems to deny any responsibility for the killings. But then he continues: "Et si sachiez bien que ce n'a pas esté par ma chevalerie, mes par mon pechié" (3:23-24). While he has just blamed misfortune for his shameful acts, he now admits that he has sinned. The terms *mescheance* and *pechié* seem contradictory to us, yet their very ambiguity is at the heart of the narrative.

Semantic analysis[2] reveals that both words, probably because of frequent proximity, have borrowed a secondary meaning from each other. *Mescheance*, originally meaning "bad fall," misfortune, can also indicate guilt; whereas *pechié*, sin, has also come to mean misfortune. The ambiguity, then, which is present in the juxtaposition of the two words, can also exist in each word taken separately. Each time we come across these words we must keep in mind this possibility. The heroes commit acts for which they admit guilt and shame, but at the same time they see them as misfortunes which "befall" them. For clarity's sake, we will use both terms in their original sense, unless otherwise stated. *Mescheance* is the theme which dominates the downward movement. It drags the heroes down to death and disaster in spite of themselves. As the story unfolds, this force will make itself known as fate or destiny, which takes on a personal form as "dame Fortune." *Mescheance* is constantly interwoven with the willful decisions and sinfun actions of the heroes, in such a way that each element adds to the other's downward pull.

Arthur concludes his conversation with Gawain by somberly predicting that ". . .les aventures del roiaume de Logres estoient si menees a fin qu'il n'en avenoit mes nule se petit non,. . ." (3:38-41). The king realizes that the great adventures of the kingdom of Logres have come to an end. As at the beginning of former adventures, Arthur announces a tournament, this time at Winchester. But he no longer expects his knights to excel in bravery and triumph in combat; he just hopes to keep them in training. So the reader is forewarned that the great days of chivalry are over. He is called upon to witness the demise of King Arthur and his realm.

At this point Lancelot is introduced into the narrative and with his appearance a foundation is laid for the following plot. During the quest for the Holy Grail Lancelot avoided Queen Guinevere. He led a chaste life, as was commanded him by the hermit who confessed him. But hardly a month has passed since his return to court, and he is more ardently in love with her than ever before. ". . .il renchei el pechié de la reine" (4:9). In these words we find again the two elements misfortune and sin, for *rencheoir*, to "fall back" (derived from *cheoir*, as in *mescheance*), seems to indicate an involuntary act. In returning to his old love, Lancelot could not help himself, he "fell." His love of the queen shows the double aspect of sin and fatefulness. As if to emphasize the latter, the author adds that the queen, even at fifty, was still the most beautiful lady in the world and regarded by all as "the fountain of all beauty." Perhaps more serious, and certainly more dangerous than their love for each other, is the fact that Lancelot has abandoned all caution. Whereas in former days they kept their love a secret, they now show it so openly that Agravain, one of Gawain's brothers who disliked Lancelot and had been watching him closely, discovers their love affair.

With Agravain's discovery, an element of suspense is introduced and a plot begins to take shape. Suspense takes the form of a spiral moving back and forth between Arthur's suspicion that Lancelot is disloyal and the return of Arthur's confidence in him. Each time a new incident shakes this restored confidence, Arthur's suspicions intensify, until finally the truth is revealed to him. The action thus describes a spiral with ever narrowing circles, winding in a downward direction. (see figure 1)

The four opening paragraphs discussed above can be regarded as the prologue to the romance. They situate it in the cycle of Round Table adventures, introduce the main characters, and lay the foundation for the plot. Moreover, they set the tone. The losses suffered in the quest and the somber presentiment of King Arthur reveal that his kingdom is crumbling. The two protagonists, Gawain and Lancelot, are introduced side by side as sinners, pursued by fate. No doubt this beginning will be of great influence on coming events. The misbehavior of the two heroes, the two most distinguished knights at the court of King Arthur, strikes an ominous note. The downward trend which is here announced runs the length of the narrative. As the story unfolds, many new elements add their force to this current which eventually drags down King Arthur and his knights.

While the reader is thus constantly made aware of the impending catastrophe, he does not know just how this will come about nor when it will take place. Hence the element of suspense, created by the spiral movement. We have seen how, in the first part of the romance, the spiral moves between Arthur's confidence in Lancelot and suspicion of his infidelity, each time getting a little closer to the final discovery and consequent breach between them. This movement continues in the second part, but on a much larger scale, for it involves two opposing parties rather than just a personal relationship. In the second half of the romance the spiral winds between peace, or at least truce, and more and more devastating wars which finally lead to total ruin.

The two movements, vertical and spiral, provide the framework for the narrative. They are closely interwoven and coincide at many points, as is shown in figure 1. While the vertical movement receives its impetus from *mescheance,* a force outside of man's reach, the spiral moves primarily on the human level. It is the result of the decisions and actions taken by the heroes. Its central theme is "honor," for this is the principle which guides their conduct.

Honor is a strong and positive force, yet from its very strength conflicts erupt. For the protagonists embrace different conventions, each prescribing its specific code of honor, its own definition of allegiance. The knight of the Round Table owes allegiance to King Arthur. The code of chivalry demands that he be ready at all times to defend his own honor as well as that of his king and his companions. As a courtly lover, however, his first loyalty should be to his lady. The code of courtly love requires that he continue to prove his love for her by brave and gallant deeds and that he come to her rescue whenever her honor is at stake. Moreover, he is also member of a family, and as such he has to defend its honor and avenge any insults received by other members of the family. It is easy to see how these different demands of honor can create conflicts. The problem of divided loyalties lies at the heart of the narrative, and is responsible for the spiraling force toward personal enmities, war, and destruction.

The author employs a number of narrative techniques to create these movements. A brief description of each of these techniques may suffice here by way of introduction.

Juxtaposition is an essential ingredient of the spiral movement. Two alternative courses of action, the opposite choices of two heroes, or two codes of conduct each demanding contrary action, are shown side by side. Their proximity brings out contrasts and similarities in a much more striking way than comparison or argument could do. Juxtaposition reveals the underlying tension which is largely responsible for the action and interaction.

The narrative device which is used to particular advantage in this romance is the technique of interlace, first pointed out by Ferdinand Lot. He has shown how many threads connect the different parts of this cycle in such a way that none of these parts forms a self-sufficient unit. Present events have their roots in the distant past, and will in their turn cast their shadows far ahead. In studying this particular romance we shall constantly be reminded that it forms an integral part of the whole of the *Cycle.* Past predictions will here be fulfilled, and acts performed in preceding parts of the *Cycle* will come to bear on these new adventures. *La Mort le Roi Artu* presents a particularly tightly knit composition, since it is the closing episode of the *Cycle.* By picking up loose ends from the past and interweaving them with new themes, the author brings many heretofore unresolved conflicts to their conclusion.

The final catastrophe is announced many times. Future events are anticipated by means of predictions, presentiments, and premonitions, and revealed in the form of visions and warnings. Repetition is effective here, for it emphasizes the inescapability of fate and imparts a sense of pervasive doom. At the same time, predictions, warnings, and visions are seldom repeated in exactly the same form. Repetitions are often varied in such a way that they show different aspects or details, which, taken together, provide the reader with increasingly more specific information as the narrative progresses.

Future happenings are also foretold in a more subtle way: by means of analogy. Analogy indicates a comparison of two things, alike in certain respects, in which one unfamiliar idea is explained by comparing it in certain of its similarities with more familiar ideas.[3] In our text, these comparisons are often implicit. Certain occurrences which at first sight seem to be gratuitous because they do not immediately contribute to the plot, appear to prepare or prefigure later events. Though the reader may not be aware of it at the time, these prefigurations serve to set the tone and prepare the mood for later, similar happenings. Together they weave a thread through the narrative, bringing out a meaning which was hidden in each separate event.

A final technique to be discussed is parallelism, a structural arrangement of paragraphs and larger units of composition by which one element of equal importance with another is similarly developed and phrased. The function of parallelism in the romance is not so much to bring out meaning as to give esthetic pleasure by creating a well-balanced bi-partite composition.

The following chapters will examine how each of the techniques mentioned above contributes to the esthetic effect of the narrative.

DIVIDED LOYALTIES
as shown by means of Juxtaposition

When we speak of juxtaposition in literature we are aware that the concept applies primarily to the realm of the visual arts. We think, for instance, of a fresco or tapestry depicting various battle scenes next to one another. In prose or poetry this spatial proximity is replaced by temporal sequence. Even when the author wants to relate several events which take place simultaneously, he can only describe them successively.[1]   In literary form then, juxtaposition appears as immediate or rapid succession.

The use of juxtaposition as a narrative device is typical for the Old French epic, where we find it not only in the paratactic sentence structure, but also in the *laisses similaires.* In his analysis of *La Chanson de Roland* Erich Auerbach says of this narrative device: "in all cases rationally organized condensations are avoided in favor of a halting, spasmodic, juxtapositive, and pro- and retrogressive method in which causal, modal, and even temporal relations are obscured."[2]

Mildred Pope distinguishes between two types of *laisses similaires:* "In the one we have set before us a repeated action, the representation of two, three, or more separate but similar acts, described each in separate but similar *laisses;* in the other the poet gives us the detailed description of one single action or emotion: . . .the act gradually revealed in its entirety, the emotion under its different aspects."[3]   An example of the first type is Oliver's threefold insistence that Roland blow his horn. His repeated summons heightens the tension of the plot, while Roland's repeated refusal reveals his pride. The second type of *laisses similaires* is illustrated in the three strophes describing Roland's death. Here repetition does not so much accentuate three different moments in time, as give us three perceptions of the same event. Each of these *laisses* stresses a different aspect or adds a fresh detail to this event, thus complementing the others. Together they provide us with a more complete picture of the state of mind in which Roland meets his death. Not always, however, do the *laisses* complement one another harmoniously. When Ganelon proposes Roland as commander of the rear guard, Roland's twofold response seems contradictory: the one stresses acceptance, the other rebellion. Logically, his two reactions cannot be reconciled. But when we see in each response an expression of the two strong emotions which Roland feels simultaneously, we realize that the two *laisses* together reveal to us the complexity of Roland's ambivalent feelings.

In musical terms, we can regard this second type of *laisses similaires* as variations upon a theme. This "thematic" mode complements the chronological order of the narrative, or, in the words of Eugène Vinaver: "chez l'auteur idéal des chansons de geste, le mouvement linéaire ou vertical se complétait sans cesse par un mouvement horizontal, la conscience du contexte immédiat par celle du contexte thématique."[4]

When we now return to *La Mort le Roi Artu,* we find there a use of juxtaposition resembling that of this latter type of *laisses similaires.* Of course, its thirteenth-century author has at his disposal a much greater variety of narrative techniques than had the twelfth-century poet. Here juxtaposition does not replace hypotaxis; the prose flows easily and logical connections between the sentences are clearly expressed. But we may say that, as in the *chanson de geste,* a thematic structure of juxtaposed statements and situations complements the narrative order of events. To find out just how the author makes use of juxtaposition and to what end, we shall analyze several passages which illustrate this narrative technique.

In the sixth chapter we find a first example in Arthur's response to Agravain who has just told him about the love affair between Lancelot and Guinevere. Pretending concern for the king's honor, Agravain proposes to set a trap for the lovers. Arthur's response to this shocking news is of interest. His first reaction is one of disbelief: "Agravain, biaus niés, ne dites jamés tel parole, car ge ne vos en creroie pas. Car ge sei bien veraiement que Lancelos nel penseroit en nule maniere" (6:23-26). Arthur thus refuses to believe Agravain and expresses confidence in Lancelot. But, after at first dismissing the rumor, he begins to doubt and continues: "et certes se il onques le pensa, force d'amors li fist fere, encontre qui sens ne reson ne puet avoir duree" (6:26-29). Now the king admits the possibility of the affair, but immediately he excuses his favorite knight, saying that the force of love is such that reason cannot resist it. Impatient, Agravain asks his uncle what he plans to do about the situation. Arthur replies: "Que voulez vos que g'en face?" (6:29-30). Agravain then urges his uncle to have the lovers watched so that they may be surprised together. To this proposal the king answers: "Fetes en ce que vos voudroiz; que ja par moi n'en seroiz destournez" (6:34-36). Satisfied, Agravain says that he asks nothing more.

The king's reaction to Agravain's story is puzzling. We can well understand Arthur's initial response to the startling news: disbelief at first, then doubt whether perhaps there is a grain of truth in it after all. What follows, however, is more difficult to comprehend. We would expect Arthur to explode in anger, or perhaps to be numb from the shock, but certainly not to be so ready to excuse him who betrayed his confidence. Such generosity on the part of the deceived husband seems improbable. Arthur's unwillingness to act upon the information perplexes us further. Only when Agravain insists and proposes a specific line of action does Arthur agree to let him carry out his plan to surprise Lancelot and Guinevere together. He gives his nephew free rein, but makes it clear that he himself will have no part of it.

This reaction on the part of a lord who has just heard that his favorite knight is deceiving him with his wife, is somewhat unbelievable. The king forgives too easily; he is too calm and too passive. Psychologically his words do not make sense to us. But we see this passage in a different light when we ask: "What does the author want to convey to the reader by means of Arthur's reply?" Such an interpretation requires a "horizontal" rather than a "vertical" reading. We then regard Arthur's answers as a series of juxtaposed statements which, coming from the king, are meant to serve us as guidelines for the interpretation of the following narrative.

The king states, first of all, that he values Lancelot highly. Of this we are reminded throughout the romance. No matter how Lancelot behaves or of what he is accused, the author never lets us forget that he is Arthur's favorite knight, respected by all. The second statement presents love as an irresistible force against which reason is powerless. It shows us the perspective in which to view the following developments. As we read how Lancelot continues to love and see the queen in spite of his devotion to King Arthur, we must remember the king's own statement on love. It presents Lancelot rather as a victim of love's power than as a knight who willfully betrays his king. Thirdly, the king does not express any desire for personal vengeance. He would have preferred not to stir things up. But he is a public figure, and Agravain's discovery of Lancelot's love for the queen makes it a matter of public concern. It is not only Arthur's honor which is at stake, but the honor of his family and his kingdom as well. He therefore cannot ignore the affair, but is obliged to efface the shame by punishment.

Juxtaposition thus brings out two themes—love and honor. Love's power is clearly stated. Honor is not explicitly mentioned, but is implied in the king's permission to his nephew to avenge him. Love and honor are the two dominant themes of the romance which are developed as the plot unfolds. In the light of the king's statements, we shall see Lancelot overpowered by love, and the king by his obligation to family and subjects. Both appear to be in the grip of forces stronger than themselves against which they are helpless. By emphasizing the power of these forces rather than the responsibility of the individual characters, the author's statements draw our attention to some of the principles which govern the society of the Round Table, and to their possible effects on the fellowship of knights.

The various conventions which rule chivalric society are often contradictory, thus creating conflicts for the heroes. Juxtaposition here serves to emphasize the dramatic tensions resulting from these conflicts. In the following episode the author juxtaposes Lancelot's two loyalties to show us the tension produced by their contrasting demands.

Lancelot does not go to Winchester in the company of his fellow knights, but follows them later. The reason is not, as

Agravain supposes, that Lancelot wants to be alone with the queen, but that he prefers to participate in the tournament incognito. En route he stays with the rich vassal of Escalot whose beautiful daughter is immediately attracted to the unknown knight. Lancelot's squire, when pressed by her, will tell her only that his master is "the best knight in the world," but he refuses to reveal Lancelot's identity. Satisfied with this answer, the maiden goes up to Lancelot and, kneeling before him, she asks: "Gentis chevaliers, done moi un don par la foi que tu doiz a la riens el monde que tu mieuz ainmes" (14:2-4). With these words, the maiden has unwittingly appealed to Lancelot's loyalty to the queen. Lancelot cannot refuse, for a favor requested in his lady's name must be granted. He therefore graciously consents: "Ha! damoisele, levez vos sus. Sachiez veraiement qu'il n'est riens en terre que ge puisse fere que ge ne feïsse por ceste requeste, car trop m'avez conjuré" (14:7-11). The girl thereupon tells him that he has just promised to wear her sleeve attached to his helmet in the tournament, and to fight for love of her. Since this is an honor which a knight customarily bestows on the lady he loves, it is immediately clear in what perilous situation Lancelot will find himself if the queen should ever hear of it. He is well aware of the serious consequences which his promise to the maiden may have. The queen would never forgive him! Yet he cannot go back on his word, for "autrement seroit il desloiax, se il ne fesoit a la damoisele ce qu'il li avoit en couvenant" (14:24-26). The disloyalty mentioned here is disloyalty to the principles of chivalry. Once a knight has given his word, he must stand by it, regardless of consequences. Lancelot is caught between the conflicting demands of two conventions, those of courtly love and those of knighthood. The precepts of courtly love have forced him to grant the damsel's request, thereby putting him in a false and misleading position in regard to the maiden. Lancelot's agreement to fight for her in the tournament is bound to make her believe that he responds to her love. When, much later, she hears that his heart belongs to another, the blow is so cruel and unexpected that it kills her.

On the other hand, Lancelot has to respect the code of chivalry. Honoring his promise as a knight puts Lancelot in a false position in regard to the queen. The code of courtly love requires that a knight continue to earn his lady's love by of bravery. By going to the tournament incognito, Lanc would distinguish himself the more, in honor of his lady, the queen. Instead, true to his promise to the maiden, he will wear the latter's sleeve and appear to do battle for her sake. While he had set out to gain honor for his lady, he will end up by provoking her jealousy. The misunderstanding will cause separation and, consequently, anguish on the part of both Guinevere and Lancelot. Thus three people will suffer as a result of Lancelot's plight. We have seen, however, that he is not to blame. The juxtaposition of the two conventions, chivalry and courtly love, and their codes of behavior, has shown that Lancelot himself is the victim of their contrary demands.

Paradox exists not only in chivalric honor, but within the all-potent force of love as well, and juxtaposition is used to define it. In a long speech addressed to Guinevere Bohort juxtaposes the destructive and the creative power of love, in an effort to persuade the queen to let Lancelot return to court. For, as Lancelot had feared, the queen has discovered the identity of the knight with the sleeve who became champion of the tournament. Deeply shaken by Lancelot's apparent disloyalty, she refuses to see him. Bohort then goes to her to plead his cousin's cause (59). First he invokes destiny, saying that it was Fortuna who brought her and Lancelot together. His words remind us of the power of fate which governs man's life. Still, although destiny determines the final outcome, man constantly has to make decisions. The queen has to make an important one at this moment. Bohort shows her the grave consequences which her answer may have. In support of his argument he quotes examples from the Bible, mythology, and literature, of men who died and were disgraced because of the woman they loved. In the same way Guinevere would be responsible for Lancelot's dishonor if she persisted in her spitefulness. But her guilt would be greater than that of the others, for, says Bohort, in Lancelot are united all the virtues by which a man can gain honor on earth, namely, "biautez et proesce, hardemenz et chevalerie, gentillesce" (59:65-66). The queen has it in her power to sustain Lancelot in his high position or to destroy him: "Dame, toutes ces vertuz poez vos tenir el cors mon seigneur si parfitement que nulle n'en faut; . . . . Mes tout einsi comme il est ores vestuz et couverz de toutes bones vertuz, tout einsi le despoilleroiz vos et desnueroiz" (59:66-68, 73-76). Courtly love can be beneficial to knighthood, since the lady's love and the knight's desire to please her bring out the best chivalric qualities, such as bravery and graciousness. On the other hand, if love remains unanswered, it can be detrimental to these knightly virtues. If Guinevere persists in her refusal to see Lancelot, she will take away "d'entre les estoiles le soleil, ce est a dire la fleur des chevaliers del monde d'entre les chevaliers le roi Artu" (59:77-79). Because Lancelot is "the sun among the stars" and "the flower of knighthood," Guinevere's decision will not only make or break her lover, it will also affect the company of the Round Table and even the whole of the realm. Thus, by means of examples, contrasts, and an appeal to the queen, Bohort juxtaposes here the creative and the destructive role of love. The latter becomes one of the dominant themes of the romance.

Bondage to the loved one is not the only allegiance which comes into conflict with loyalty to the king and the principles of knighthood. Family loyalty combines with it to further undermine the fellowship of the Round Table. This is first illustrated in the decision of Lancelot's relatives to leave court in search of their cousin rather than stay with the queen who accuses Lancelot of infidelity. But instead of simply juxtaposing their different loyalties, the author clearly establishes priorities here. As Bohort takes his leave, he says to the queen: "Et sachiez veraiement, dame, que nos n'eüssons mie tant demoré en cest païs comme nos avons, se por l'amor de mon seigneur ne fust, ne il n'i eüst pas tant demoré aprés la queste del Seint Graal lors por vos" (39:59-64). According to Bohort, the cousins' loyalty to Lancelot is stronger than their devotion to King Arthur, in the same way that Lancelot's loyalty to the queen has precedence over his attachment to the king.

The cousins are unsuccessful in their search. They go to the tournament at Tanebourc, hoping to see Lancelot there, but he does not appear. King Arthur, who had come to the tournament with the same expectation, is equally disappointed. He announces that another tournament will take place a month later, at Camelot. He then invites Bohort and his companions to return to court with him, but they refuse, saying that they will not rest until they have news of Lancelot (44:2-4). A few days later Arthur again requests that Bohort and his party join him, but again they refuse, this time in much stronger terms: "il distrent qu'il n'iroient pas ne jamés n'i enterroient a nul jor, devant ce qu'il seüssent veraies noveles de Lancelot" (44:32-35). The next day both parties go their way, with Gawain joining Bohort, out of friendship for Lancelot. Bohort's words and the cousins' subsequent departure are a first indication that obligations to family and to King Arthur are on a collision course. The divisive power of family loyalty is, of course, exemplified later in the romance in the person of Gawain, whose fanatic vindication of the family honor causes the dissolution of the Round Table fellowship.

Even King Arthur himself, who embodies the spirit of chivalry, is torn by inner conflict. After the discovery of the love affair, Lancelot manages to escape, but Guinevere is condemned to death by fire. Lancelot assembles a rescue party which attacks the knights assigned to guard the fire. He saves the queen, but the cost in lives is high. In the fighting three of Arthur's nephews are killed, one of whom, Gaheriet, by Lancelot himself who did not recognize him. Overcome by grief, Arthur holds council with his barons. He tells them that Lancelot is responsible for the loss of his *"ami charnel"* and asks their advice on how to revenge the dishonor brought upon his family. King Yon rises and says that, as the king's liege man, he has to consider both the honor of the king and of the realm. He agrees that the king's honor demands revenge. Yet he counsels against it, for Lancelot's relatives are known to be excellent knights and to attack them would imperil the kingdom. Juxtaposition comes here close to comparison, as King Yon weighs Arthur's obligations to his family against those to his knights. In King Yon's opinion the latter should have priority. The safety of the realm and the preservation of the fellowship are more important than the loss and dishonor suffered by the king and his family. King Yon, however, is quickly silenced, accused of cowardice. Encouraged by his other barons, Arthur decides to avenge his dishonor against those who have deprived him of his beloved nephew (104). And so, in the name of family loyalty, a war is declared which will split the fellowship of the Round Table into two opposing parties.

During Arthur's siege of the castle of Joyous Guard where Lancelot and the queen have taken refuge, Lancelot makes a last effort toward reconciliation. He sends a damsel to the king with the following message: if the king has begun war because of the queen, he, Lancelot, is ready to defend himself against Arthur's best knight; if, on the other hand, the king has declared war because of the death of his nephews, he should know that those nephews were more to blame than Lancelot. But, if he stands by his decision to do battle, Lancelot will defend himself as best he can (109:21-50). As Arthur debates with Gawain on how to respond to Lancelot's message, it becomes clear that the death of his nephews is the real issue of the war, and that Lancelot's "treason" with the queen has receded to the background. For Gawain there is no dilemma—his great love and admiration for Lancelot have changed into hate with the death of his brother Gaheriet. The king, however, cannot forget that Lancelot has done more for him than any other knight. He balances, as it were, the right and the wrong which Lancelot has done to him. He finds that the latter outweighs the former: "mes au derrien le m'a trop vendu chierement, car il m'a tolu mes amis charnex et ceus que je plus amoie, fors vous tant solement" (110:28-30). Arthur concludes therefore that he will fight to the death. Thus it is vindication of the family honor which makes Arthur decline Lancelot's peace offer and which initiates the fatal war.

Sometime later, after Lancelot has saved Arthur's life and the Pope has ordered the king to take the queen back, peace seems to be a real possibility. Again Lancelot's merit and "treason" are put in a balance. On the one side Lancelot reminds the king how he saved the kingdom for him on the day he conquered Galeholt. He also recalls to Gawain that he freed him from the Dolorous Tower where Karados the Great had imprisoned him. Certainly both owe him gratitude. But for Gawain all this is outweighed by the death of his brothers: "Lancelot, fait mesire Gauvains, onques ne feïstes riens pour moi que vous ne m' aïés moult cher vendu au daerrain; car vous m'avés si dolerousement adamagié de ciaus que je plus amoie que nostres parentés en est del tout abaissiés et je en sui honnis; et pour ce ne porroit il mie avoir pais entre moi et vous. . ." (119:124-131). And so, while the king is now inclined to make peace with Lancelot, Gawain persists in his vengeance. He will not rest until Lancelot has paid with his life for the killing of his brothers.

The examples discussed so far concerned critical situations in which conflicts arose from the knights' obligation to obey several contradictory codes of behavior. However, the tensions which thus broke out into the open are ever present, reflected in the character of each protagonist. Again the author uses the technique of juxtaposition to show the different loyalties which exist side by side in a single character. The protagonists are not divided into heroes and villains; they all unite to some extent the qualities of both.

This is most evident in the case of Lancelot, the principal character in the romance. While he is absent from court, banished by the queen, she is—unjustly—accused of poisoning the brother of Mador de la Porte. When Mador demands satisfaction, none of the knights assembled wants to do battle in behalf of the queen, for all believe her guilty. At the last moment Lancelot arrives and offers to defend the queen's honor. Mador is an excellent knight, but Lancelot proves to be superior. When he finally has Mador at his mercy, he spares his life, because he has recognized in him a former comrade in arms. The combat thus ends on a happy note, and Lancelot is welcomed back at court with great joy. The king embraces him and Gawain unlaces his helmet. All rejoice, and the author exclaims: "Lors poïssiez veoir entor lui si grant joie que de greigneur n'orroiz vos jamés parler" (85:16-17). Lancelot has distinguished himself as a courteous defender of the queen's honor, and as a brave and generous knight. Immediately after this triumphant hour, however, he relapses into his old sin. Reconciled with Guinevere, he loves her so passionately and recklessly that even Gawain notices it. Word reaches the king who promises to avenge this insult. But just then a knight arrives with news from the tournament of Karahes. He tells the king that those of Sorelois and the Terre Gaste have lost, and that Lancelot has triumphed over all. Thus Lancelot's indiscreet behavior as a lover is flanked by two heroic deeds which show his unsurpassed valor. This ambiguity in his character is succinctly expressed by the king as he cries out: "Ha! Dex, quel douleur et quel domage quant en si preudome se herberja onques traïson!" (87:19-21).

Some time later, in his rescue of the queen, Lancelot, as we have seen above, accidentally kills one of his best friends, Gaheriet. While obeying the demand of courtly love to save his lady, he thus violates the bond of chivalry by killing one of his own comrades. This not only brings him into conflict with the fellowship of knights, but it also calls down upon him the wrath of King Arthur's family. We see Lancelot here at the lowest point of his career, for this incident sets off the war which will lead to the ultimate catastrophe. Yet, immediately following this episode, the author shows how Lancelot is beloved by his own people. They receive him as if he were God, and with more splendor than they would have bestowed on King Arthur himself. It seems that the author does not want to leave in our mind the image of Lancelot as a sinner whose unchivalric behavior causes a disastrous war. He quickly juxtaposes another image, that of the beloved and honored lord. As if to balance the moment when Lancelot appears to be most guilty, the author heaps on him the highest praise. He compares him to King Arthur, symbol of knighthood, and even to God!

In a similar way, Gawain's outrageous family loyalty is—at least to some extent—balanced by his bravery. Defeated by Lancelot, he lies seriously wounded, as a result of his stubborn pride. But the author does not keep him long in this humiliating position. As he did with Lancelot earlier, he immediately takes pains to elevate him. Although Gawain has lost, Bohort expresses admiration for his endurance: "Si ai tant veu de vos deus que vos estes li dui meilleur chevalier del monde" (158:54-55). All marvel that Gawain has lasted so long against Lancelot, who is the best knight in the world and, besides, twenty-one years younger than Gawain.

Soon afterwards, when the Romans invade the land, Gawain has an opportunity to rehabilitate himself. He fights well, killing the emperor's nephew. In the ensuing melee he is dealt a blow on the helmet which reopens his wound and will prove fatal. This wound, originally inflicted by Lancelot in combat, is a visible token of Gawain's pride, of the fact that he valued his own and his family's honor more than the unity of the Round Table and the safety of the realm. Yet he now gives his life for that realm. Thus the head wound symbolizes his divided loyalties: to his family, and to the fellowship of knights and his king.

Gawain dies bravely, in defense of the king; all agree that "s'il ne fust einsi preudom li Romain n'eüssent pas esté veincu" (163:15-17). The hero whose fanatic vengeance has split and fatally weakened the kingdom, dies defending that kingdom, and is deeply mourned by all. The king praises him as a man who surpassed everyone in goodness, and the people lament because "mesire Gauvains avoit esté li chevaliers el monde plus amés de diverses gens" (173:11-13). A final tribute comes from the ladies in the person of the lady of Beloé who throws herself upon his body, exclaiming: "Ha! Messire Gauvain, tant est granz domages de vostre mort, meesmement as dames et as damoiseles!" (174:15-17). She then professes her love for him and is thereupon slain by her jealous husband.

All this praise heaped upon Gawain in the wake of his death provides an esthetic balance to the blame he earned for his long-lasting, outrageous pride. In some measure, it serves to redeem him. It does not, however, efface his sin. Pride and virtue exist side by side in his character. Blinded by his desire to avenge the honor of his family, he is guilty of dividing the fellowship of knights. But at the same time, he is and remains one of its most excellent knights, brave, beloved—a "father" to the people.

Juxtaposition serves not only to show the different sides of one man's character. Often two persons are presented side by side in order to bring out contrasts or similarities between them. This device is applied in particular to Lancelot and Gawain, the two protagonists. We saw them in the opening paragraphs introduced as two sinners, pursued by fate. In the first part of the romance the friendship between them, Arthur's two best knights, is emphasized. But with the death of Gaheriet Gawain's loyal friendship turns into bitter hostility. From this point on the two knights, now opponents, are often shown to us side by side, sometimes to draw our attention to common traits, but more often to contrasting qualities.

The first major outbreak between Lancelot's party and that of King Arthur and Gawain occurs before the castle of Joyous Guard. As the balance is made up after the first day of battle, all agree that both Gawain and Lancelot have won the prize for that day: "si donerent de celui jour tout le pris a monseignor Gauvain et a Lancelot et distrent que c'estoient li dui chevalier qui mielz l'avoient fet en la bataille. . ." (114:15-18). They equal each other in bravery. Gawain refuses a truce, however, and as the war intensifies Lancelot is often favorably compared to Gawain. The siege of Gaunes is not going well for Arthur, and Gawain proposes a single combat between him and

Lancelot to settle the issue. The king tries to dissuade him, pointing out that Lancelot is the most proven and "chosen" valorous knight in the world. But Gawain is not to be stopped: ". . .car ge le hé si mortelment que ge voudroie mieuz morir que ge ne me meïsse en aventure de lui ocirre" (146:50-52). To this mortal hate of Gawain, Lancelot opposes love for his old friend. He dreads fighting him, "non mie por poor que j'aie de lui, mes por ce que ge l'amoie si que ja ne queïsse assembler a lui cors contre cors en bataille" (145:49-51). Bohort finds it remarkable that "si l'amés de grant cuer, et il vous het mortelment" (145:74-75). To which Lancelot answers that his love is greater than Gawain's hate ever can be.

Somewhat more subtle is the comparison between the two in a following encounter of the opponents. As they approach King Arthur's party, Lancelot tells Bohort to descend from his horse out of respect for the king. Bohort protests, but Lancelot insists that he dismount for love of the king, even though they are enemies (147:14-15). His great courtesy impresses the king and stands in sharp contrast to Gawain's subsequent rude behavior. When Lancelot addresses the king, politely and even humbly, Gawain jumps forward and answers in the king's place. Still, Lancelot persists in his peace efforts. Instead of mentioning all he did for the king, he courteously recalls all the king and Gawain have done for him. This, he says, makes it difficult for him to now take up arms against Gawain. Even though Lancelot has the strategic advantage, he goes out of his way to pursue peace. He offers to become Gawain's liege man with his family, and to go into exile for as long as ten years. Finally he swears that he did not knowingly kill Gaheriet. The king, now convinced of Lancelot's innocence, presses his nephew to accept this most generous offer. Gawain, however, remains implacable. He maintains that his honor can be saved only by a fight to the death. But now even his own party sides with Lancelot. Both Arthur and Ywain blame Gawain. It has gradually become clear to all that Lancelot has justice on his side. Gawain's pride and *outrecuidance* are contrasted with Lancelot's generosity and humility (149:10).

The effect of these alternating episodes is in the first place esthetically pleasing. It gives rhythm and variety to the narrative. Juxtaposition further reveals that many conflicts find their origin in divided loyalties. In the character of Lancelot we have seen most clearly the tension between lover and knight. Lancelot's faithfulness to his lady is the primary cause leading to the breaking up of the Round Table fellowship. As Lancelot is banished from court, his relatives leave also, out of sympathy with their cousin and brother. In this manner, family loyalty brings about the first major division within the fellowship, and former comrades become enemies.

Gawain, the perfect knight, becomes a fanatic, in relentless pursuit of revenge. Family loyalty overrides his obligations to chivalric society. To the honor of his family he sacrifices friendship, fellowship, and even the peace of the realm. King Arthur too lets family sentiments interfere with the principles of knighthood and the well-being of his kingdom by siding with his nephew. He allows him to perpetuate the war in spite of repeated warnings of doom and destruction. He also leaves his nephew Mordred in charge without consulting his barons. Blood relationship rather than the interest of the people seems to determine his choice. His ill-advised decisions lead to the final split among his barons and to civil war.

The fellowship of the Round Table is ruled by the code of chivalry. It is broken up by forces from within because other loyalties undermine the bond which links the knights and their leader, King Arthur. Faithfulness to the loved one and to family takes its toll upon the comradeship of knights until this crumbles and finally disintegrates.

In the introduction to his edition of *La Mort le Roi Artu*, Jean Frappier says of the characters: "Les personnages ne se classent plus en élus et en réprouvés; ils n'ont plus cette valeur d'exemples que la *Queste* conférait aux différents chercheurs du Saint-Graal; à travers des alternances de grandeur et de faiblesse, ils sont bons et mauvais à la fois, en eux-mêmes, sans correspondance symbolique avec des essences supra-terrestres. *La Mort Artu* se cantonne dans la peinture d'une réalité morale qui ne dépasse pas l'homme."[5] According to Frappier, the fact that good and bad are present in a single character points to a psychological realism. This, however, is questionable. It is true that the characters here do not symbolize superhuman forces. But neither do they act as individuals who are masters of their own lives. Instead they seem to be in the power of a number of conventions which govern chivalric society. Each of these conventions has its code of behavior which prescribes how to act in certain circumstances, and the characters often appear as a sort of "battleground" on which different loyalties combat each other.

The technique of juxtaposition is most appropriate to express these conflicts, for it reflects in literary form precisely the way in which the various allegiances exist side by side in the heroes' minds and lives. It reveals to us clearly the dilemma in which the characters are caught. The opposing loyalties seldom offer a clear choice between alternatives. Although there is often a weighing of different lines of conduct, the outcome is not so much the result of a personal decision as of the prevalence of one code over another. No compromise is possible. Faithfulness to the loved one and to family weakens the unity of the knights with their leader, King Arthur. And so King Arthur's fellowship ultimately collapses because it was built on insoluble tensions.

PLOT WEAVING, SUSPENSE, AND COHESION
as Results of the Interlace Pattern

As the reader follows the heroes on their final adventures, he encounters a confusing series of seemingly disconnected episodes. Not only do numerous adventures alternate and continually interrupt one another, they also present a variety of themes which leave an impression of chaos. Yet a closer look reveals internal relationships which create order and cohesion among the diverse episodes and themes. The establishing of such links is the effect of interlacing. In order to trace the origin and development of the interlace design, we must first turn to the visual arts.

The design dates back as far as prehistoric Mesopotamia and is, in one form or another, characteristic of the art of all races. Whatever its precise origin may have been, authorities agree on its universal application.[1] It appears in a variety of places at different periods of history: in the architectural monuments of certain East Christian sects, in the stylized patterns of Islamic art, and in Anglo-Saxon art of the seventh and eighth centuries.[2] In the Middle Ages we see it in Romanesque sculpture and in manuscript illuminations, where it takes the form of the ribbon ornament.

The ribbon ornament is a geometric design, consisting of several bands plaited together to form a braid or rope pattern. "Interlace is made when the bands are turned back on themselves to form knots or breaks that interrupt, so to speak, the linear flow of the bands."[3] That is to say that the design has neither a center, nor a beginning or end. Yet the pattern is cohesive: tight interlacing integrates the various bands into a unified design.[4] The characteristics of this pattern are repetition, coincidence, and circularity. It conveys movement and vigor, but a highly and expertly controlled vigor, which suggests to some critics spiritual questing, a desire to transcend a divisive reality.[5]

Examples of a very complex interlace design are the decorated manuscript initials.[6] Two different patterns can here be distinguished: one is the geometric pattern discussed above, the other takes off from it in the shape of stylized plants and animals. These offshoots can in their turn endlessly expand, producing a flowering curve which follows the line of a coiling spiral.[7] In later manuscript decorations, for instance in the thirteenth-century Lindsey Psalter, these spirals intertwine with each other as well as with the ribbon design in such a way as to form a highly sophisticated and intricate composition.

Authorities in the fields of both art and literature have noted the correspondence between the interlace design in the visual arts and in the composition of medieval prose and poetry.[8] Wilhelm Worringer mentions "the very peculiar interlacing of words and sentences in early Northern poetry and its artful chaos of interrelated ideas."[9] Eugène Vinaver finds the combination of acentricity and cohesion back in the cyclic romances. More than that, he says: "the 'morphology' and the 'syntax' of Romanesque motifs have been defined in terms almost directly applicable to the narrative devices of thirteenth-century romance writers;" thus "the 'formation of sequences' recalls the formation of 'threads' in a cyclic narrative."[10]

It was Ferdinand Lot,[11] who, in 1918, first pointed out the importance of *entrelacement* in the composition of the thirteenth-century *Vulgate Cycle.* He examined in particular the *Lancelot en prose,* which comprises the last three branches of the *Cycle,* namely the *Lancelot* proper, *La Queste del Saint Graal,* and *La Mort le Roi Artu.* In its interlaced structure he found an argument to demonstrate what was, for him, a convincing single authorship. Even if one rejects Lot's theory, his discovery of interlace remains a valuable contribution to the study of these thirteenth-century romances.

When Lot set out to analyze certain parts of the *Cycle,* he soon found that it was practically impossible to divide the material, outside of the three major segments: "C'est qu'il était difficile et même impossible d'opérer de véritables subdivisions.

Aucune aventure ne forme un tout se suffisant à lui-même.
D'une part des épisodes antérieurs, laissés provisoirement de
côté, y prolongent des ramifications, d'autre part des épisodes
subséquents, proches ou lointains, y sont amorcés. C'est un
enchevêtrement systématique. De ce procédé de 'l'entrelacement' les exemples se présent sous la plume."[12]   Nothing is
superfluous or arbitrary, and every episode serves to prepare
another. Lot compares the text to a tapestry where the threads
are interwoven in such a way that one cannot cut through the
fabric anywhere without unraveling all of it. In the romances
a theme is brought out, then dropped, to be taken up later, just
as a thread appears, disappears, and reappears in the fabric. In
this way early episodes serve to anticipate later ones. New
themes appear simultaneously with older ones or in the intervening episodes. They have a specific function in their particular
place in the narrative, for not only do they present new topics,
they also illuminate or illustrate the themes with which they
intertwine.

What is the effect of this interweaving, other than a tightly
knit narrative structure?   In the first place, it produces variety.
Ariosto's *Orlando Furioso* may serve as illustration. In his color-
ful analysis of this work, Henri Hauvette[13] compares the author
to a musician who plays in different registers in quick succession.
The result is a richly-nuanced composition, full of contrasts and
surprises.   Another effect is that of heightened tension, created
by the suspension of a theme just when the reader's curiosity has
reached its highest peak. Ariosto himself, in discussing his work,
claims to have aimed mostly for variety: "varier les mets réveille
l'appétit."[14]   The alternating themes and moods—tender, moving, sad, gallant, comic—result in a pleasant harmony. This
multiple composition is given some unity by the tone of the
narrative, the somewhat detached irony of the poet. According
to Hauvette, unity is thus imposed from without. Apparently
he found no themes in the narrative itself which gave coherence
to the various elements. Hauvette shows a composition which
is esthetically pleasing and creates suspense through a variety of
moods and themes, but which possesses no other unifying element than a superficial one, alien to the narrative itself. Thus
the role of interlace here is limited.

An example of a more intricate interlace pattern is

Spenser's *Faerie Queene.* In her discussion of the interlaced adventures of the various heroes, Rosemond Tuve examines in detail the character of the "intervening episodes" and their contribution to the narrative.[15]   The intervening episode may introduce an entirely new theme, it may be a flashback or elaboration, or it may supply background.   If the latter is the case, "it will turn out to carry onward some second 'new' theme as well as the first one which needed the background; and from that we come back, not to precisely what we left, but to something we understand differently because of what we have since seen."[16] Multiplicity is characteristic of the interlaced structure, in which not only adventures, but also a number of themes are interwoven.   As the story unfolds, new themes appear and are in their turn developed.   ". . .we are dealing with a design wherein pattern slowly takes shape rather than with a design wherein a theme is stated and variants develop it."[17]   It is obvious that the interlace which Tuve found in the *Faerie Queene* is of a much more sophisticated nature than the pattern of the *Orlando Furioso.*   Its role here is essential to the narrative itself, for it develops the leading themes and contributes to the weaving of the plot.

An effect of interlacing in the Arthurian Prose Cycle is, as Vinaver notes, ". . .the feeling that each initial adventure can be extended into the past and each final adventure into the future by a further lenghtening of the narrative threads.   Any theme can reappear after an interval so as to stretch the whole fabric still further until the reader loses every sense of limitation in time or space."[18]   This tendency to infinity is an effect of amplification, either in the sense of a reminder or anticipation, or as a change of theme, "but with the implied assurance that the narration would eventually be resumed at the point at which it was interrupted."[19]   If a theme so amplified is pursued simultaneously with one or more other themes, they have to alternate and produce an interlace pattern.   Far from being artificially imposed, as was the case in *Orlando,* there is here an interior coherence of the subtlest kind, which "is not conveyed, as most modern readers would expect, through explanatory observations and discourses, but through the amplification and expansion of the matter itself."[20]

Relationships then, are not spelled out for us in terms of

cause and effect; it is up to the reader to infer these from the particular place which a certain event or theme occupies in regard to the narrative as a whole and to neighboring themes. The reader also needs an excellent memory, for only if the various themes are simultaneously present in his mind can he discover internal relationships and coherence. But he will be amply rewarded when he sees a pattern taking shape out of the multitude of episodes and adventures.

Such is, indeed, the case for the reader of *La Mort le Roi Artu,* where interlacing shows many of the characteristics and effects mentioned above. The interlace pattern here is especially varied in the first part of the romance which deals with the love affair between Lancelot and Guinevere and its discovery. Here the episodes of the maiden of Escalot and of the Poisoned Apple are interwoven with each other as well as with other events. Before we can examine the relationship between these episodes, the Poisoned Apple incident must be briefly related. It takes place during Lancelot's absence from court. As Lancelot had feared, the queen has heard about the maiden of Escalot and believes him to be unfaithful. When he finally returns to court, she refuses to see him. Lancelot then leaves again immediately. One day after his departure, the queen is dining with the knights of the Round Table. Someone had given her an apple which she now offers to the knight seated next to her, the brother of Mador de la Porte. Immediately upon biting into it, he falls dead. It is clear that the apple was poisoned, and, since all have seen the queen hand it to her table partner, the evidence against her is convincing. However, the apple was given to the queen by a knight who hated Gawain and hoped to kill him. He had expected her to offer the apple to Gawain as the most honorable member of the company. But because this took place behind the scenes as it were, nobody is aware of the real culprit and appearances are against the queen. When in the following episode Mador de la Porte arrives and demands satisfaction for the death of his brother, nobody steps forward to defend the queen, not even the faithful Gawain.

The two stories of the Maiden of Escalot and the Poisoned Apple together make up the greater part of the first half of the romance (See Figures 2 & 3). The Maiden of Escalot adventure is divided into five episodes, beginning in paragraph 12 and

terminating in paragraph 73.[21]   Interwoven with it initially are
tournaments and court episodes.   In paragraph 62 a new story
line is introduced with the incident of the Poisoned Apple. This
is divided into three parts which alternate with the Escalot episodes, culminating in the reconciliation of Lancelot and the
queen in paragraph 85.

The question now arises: what is the significance of this
interlace pattern for the narrative and what are its effects upon
the reader?   At the simplest level, it is esthetically pleasing.
The narrative moves back and forth between the adventures of
Lancelot, the queen, the king, Gawain, and Lancelot's relatives.
As we follow each in his turn, the scene shifts in and out between
Escalot, the court, the field of combat, and the forest. We have
seen that the alternating of the adventures of different heroes is
a common procedure in the courtly romance. It provides variety
and it heightens the tension. However, in this romance the role
of interlacing goes far beyond these obvious effects; it is essential
to the narrative itself. Its function is three-fold: it contributes to
the weaving of the plot by developing the leading themes, it
creates a double movement of suspense, and at the same time it
reveals the omnipotence of fate in the lives of the heroes.

Two of the three main themes are present from the beginning, carried over from the preceding romances: chivalry and
love. Both are found in the person of Lancelot who owes loyalty
to King Arthur as well as to his lady, the queen. These themes
are developed and clarified by interlacing. They are carried on
simultaneously: while the love theme dominates the Escalot adventure and the theme of chivalry is prevalent in the various
tournaments, both themes are embodied in the court episodes.
In the narrative the tournament and court episodes are flanked
by Escalot episodes in such a way that their intertwining clearly
illustrates the inseparability of Lancelot's two loyalties (Figure
2).   Their relationship is shown in three places where the two
themes intersect, like threads which form a knot.

This happens first in the initial Escalot episode where, as
was noted earlier, Lancelot is caught between his two loyalties
as a result of which one person will die and two others will suffer. The conflict suggests a collision course. And in fact, at the
second point of intersection, the love theme is in the ascendant.

This takes place when Lancelot, finally recovered from his wounds, wants to return to court (58-62). Convinced of his infidelity, the queen refuses to see him and Lancelot decides to leave again in the hope that his absence may change her mind. Thus his love for Guinevere prolongs Lancelot's separation from Arthur and his fellow knights and keeps him from participating in their chivalric exploits. The third meeting of the two themes appears to be a reconciliation of Lancelot's two loyalties. When he fights Mador de la Porte to save the queen's honor, he puts his knightly virtues in the service of his lady (82-85). It is a moment of harmony and relief. Lancelot has demonstrated his complete loyalty to the queen by coming to her rescue without knowledge of her actual role in the Poisoned Apple affair. He comes to her defense without a question. In combat Lancelot shines once again as a superior fighter. He is generous as well as brave, for when he has Mador at his mercy, he spares the life of his former fellow knight. Lancelot's victory is proof of the queen's innocence. The lovers are reunited and both Arthur and Gawain warmly welcome Lancelot back at court. However, this happy interlude lasts only a fleeting moment. Lancelot's imprudent love for Guinevere leads to a definite break with King Arthur and divides the fellowship into two opposing factions. Love triumphs over chivalry as Lancelot fights his former fellow knights in defense of his lady, the queen.

While these two themes wind through the entire sequence of events, a third theme is introduced somewhat later in the person of Bohort. In Bohort we see family loyalty in conflict with loyalty to the king and the queen. Twice Bohort leaves court to search for his cousin Lancelot, in spite of the insistence of the queen and the king that he remain with them. In the interlace pattern the three themes meet, part, and intersect again, tracing thereby the outline of the coming catastrophe.

The interlace pattern also contributes to the development of the story. Here applies Rosemond Tuve's observation: "But events connected by entrelacement are not juxtaposed; they are interlaced, and when we get back to our first character he is not where we left him as we finished his episode, but in the place of psychological state or condition of meaningfulness to which he has been pulled by the events occurring in following episodes written about someone else."[22] During Lancelot's prolonged absence from court events take place which will affect him on his return. These events provoke speculations on the part of both King Arthur and Queen Guinevere with regard to Lancelot's loyalty to each of them. Their feelings take them in opposite directions, for the same incidents which reassure the king, produce misgivings in the mind of the queen, and vice versa. Their respective oscillations between confidence and suspicion create a double movement of suspense (represented in figure 3 by two vertical curves).

As we enter the first Escalot episode, all is well between Lancelot and Guinevere, but Agravain's gossip about Lancelot and the queen has sown doubt in Arthur's mind concerning Lancelot's faithfulness. In the following Escalot episode Gawain, in search of his friend Lancelot, arrives at the maiden's home. The encounter reveals to Gawain that Lancelot was the unknown champion of the tournament at Winchester and that it was he who wore the maiden's sleeve. When Lancelot's absence from court continues, Gawain tells the king that he is surely detained by the maiden at Escalot. This is merely a conjecture on Gawain's part, for in reality, as the reader knows, Lancelot is recovering from his wound at the home of the maiden's aunt. Gawain's false report marks a turning point in the feelings of both the king and the queen: it reassures the king, but it turns the queen's love into hate. She remains implacable until the arrival of the boat with the maiden's body brings evidence that there was no substance to Gawain's story. In the letter which is found on her, the girl explains that she dies of her unrequited love of Lancelot. This removes the queen's suspicions of her lover's infidelity, and so the path is cleared for their reconciliation. Lancelot's rescue then brings about a happy ending to their long separation.

Meanwhile, Arthur's renewed faith in Lancelot is seriously shaken by his sister, Morgan le Fay. She receives the king in her magic castle and has him spend the night in the same room where Lancelot once was locked up and where he depicted his adventures on the wall. They clearly reveal his love for the queen. Morgan's comments that Lancelot has loved the queen since he was knighted upset Arthur even more (52:33-38). However, in spite of this convincing testimony, the king is rather easily reassured once again when he returns to court and hears that Lancelot came back, but left again immediately after his arrival. He reasons that Lancelot certainly would have stayed longer if he indeed loved Guinevere. Finally Arthur's peace is rudely shattered and this time permanently, when the lovers are found together. At this point the tensions between the king and Lancelot on one side and between the queen and Lancelot on the other side culminate in a reunion of the lovers and a complete break between Lancelot and the king. With Lancelot's return to court, relationships are out in the open and the suspense sustained throughout the preceding episodes has momentarily come to a halt.

While the interweaving of several adventures produces tension between conflicting themes, it reveals at the same time an inner coherence between the various events. The most subtle and at once the most effective contribution of the interlace pattern in this romance is that it makes us gradually become aware of a unifying theme which runs like a red thread through the whole sequence of events. This theme is to be found in *mescheance,* or fate (in Figure 3 the happenings which reveal its presence are underlined).

In the Poisoned Apple incident we have seen the queen stand accused of a murder which she had not committed. The significance of this episode in the narrative is not immediately clear to us. Of course, it prepares Lancelot's rescue, but the incident itself seems gratuitous, a freak accident of which not only the poisoned knight, but also the queen is the hapless victim. It does, however, not stand alone, isolated from other occurrences. The Poisoned Apple story is interwoven with other episodes, in particular with the story of the Maiden of Escalot, in such a way that both are present in our mind at the same time. Taken together, they assume a new meaning. In the final Escalot episode which is flanked by the second and third Poisoned Apple episodes, a little boat brings to shore the body of the maiden who died for the love of Lancelot. We see here side by side two innocent victims: the Maiden of Escalot, dead because of Lancelot, and the brother of Mador de la Porte, dead because of the queen. Their epitaphs bear witness to this: "Ici gist Gaheriz li Blans de Karaheu, li Freres Mador de la Porte, que la reine fist morir par venim" (63:11-13), and: "Ici Damoisele d'Escalot qui por l'amor de Lancelot morut" 9). Yet, although Lancelot and the queen are in a way res

ble for these deaths, neither is guilty of murder. We know that
the queen is innocent, and we know also that Lancelot was
caught between the opposite demands of two conventions and
did not purposely mislead the maiden. Whereas the Poisoned
Apple story, regarded by itself, seems to be a pure accident, the
fact that it is interwoven with another story in which a similar
death without guilt occurs removes its accidental character. Together, the two stories make us aware of a force beyond the
heroes' reach which dominates their actions and decides the
final outcome. This force is an evil one, for it claims the lives of
innocent victims—the maiden and the brother of Mador—and
threatens the reputations of Lancelot and the queen as well.

It is interesting to note that Gawain is the instrument of
fate in both stories.[23] While Lancelot and Guinevere are instrumental in the fates of respectively the maiden of Escalot and the
brother of Mador de la Porte, their fates in turn appear to be
guided through the unwitting mediation of Gawain. Gawain
attributes Lancelot's absence to a love for the maiden at Escalot.
We know this to be a false explanation. But the queen has over-
heard the conversation between Gawain and the king and, convinced of her lover's infidelity, she refuses to receive him when
he returns some time later. Gawain's lighthearted remark thus
causes anguish to both Lancelot and the queen, and a long
separation of the lovers. And the poisoned apple which Guinevere offered Mador's brother was in fact intended for Gawain
by a knight who hated him. So, indirectly, Gawain is the cause
of the other's death. In the two incidents of the Maiden of Escalot and the Poisoned Apple Gawain unwittingly helps fate to
create havoc for both Lancelot and the queen. At a time when
he is still Lancelot's best friend, his fateful role already fore-
shadows their later hostile relationship.

Still other events take place, seemingly accidental, but
which, seen in combination with the episodes discussed, serve
to bring out the presence of a hidden force in the lives of the
heroes, in particular in that of Lancelot. Twice Lancelot fails
to appear at a tournament which he wanted to attend. He is
absent from the tournament of Tanebourc because of the deep
wound he received at the tournament of Winchester. This wound
was inflicted by his cousin Bohort, who had not recognized
Lancelot in the stranger in borrowed armor. When, much later,

Bohort learns that it was he who wounded Lancelot, he is greatly distressed. In the light of the Escalot adventure with which this incident is interwoven, we see Lancelot as the victim and Bohort as the unwitting instrument of fate. While Lancelot's first absence occurs between the first two Escalot episodes, his second absence from a tournament is set between the first two Poisoned Apple episodes (64-66). Lancelot, who had wandered in the forest since he left court, sends his squire to get him a shield and suit of armor in preparation for the tournament at Camelot. As he is resting near a fountain, he is wounded in the thigh by one of the king's hunters who aimed at a deer. This accident prevents him from going to the tournament and rejoining his comrades. A mere coincidence, it would seem; the heroes call it *mescheance:* mishap or misfortune. But it is not an isolated incident. The very repetition of these mishaps and their proximity to one another reveal instead an evil force at work. We may call this force fate or destiny. Fate is ever present; not only is it openly recognized in the form of predictions and warnings, but it also interferes in the heroes' lives in the disguise of accidents and misunderstandings. It brings frustration, misery, and ruin upon them in spite of their bravery and good intentions.

Interweaving occurs not only within the limits of the romance. It is very effective in binding together the many parts of the *Vulgate Cycle.* When we regard *La Mort le Roi Artu* in the broader context of the *Lancelot en prose,* we see that earlier episodes, left aside for awhile, are here taken up again, while new themes are introduced simultaneously. Past events have cast their shadows far ahead to influence the present adventures.[24]

An example occurs in the passages discussed where Morgan le Fay shows Arthur Lancelot's wall paintings (48-55). King Arthur, lost in the forest, prepares to set up camp for the night, when he hears the sound of a horn. He sends one of his knights to ask for hospitality and is received with marvelous splendor and luxury by Morgan and a hundred maidens and knights, all richly dressed. He does not recognize his sister, but it is suggested that she has expected and prepared this meeting: "Et lors commencierent damoiseles a aporter mes, comme s'il fussent bien porveü de la venue le roi et de touz ses compaignons un mois devant" (49:5-7). After dinner the maidens escort the king to his bedroom, the same room where Lancelot had stayed before. All this is according to the scheme of Morgan, who hates Lancelot. Her hatred dates far back into the past and is founded in jealousy. She has always bitterly resented Lancelot's preference for the queen. Twice she had him imprisoned, but both times he escaped. Now Arthur's visit offers her an opportunity for revenge: she will alert the king to Lancelot's love for Guinevere.

She goes about this in a very cunning way, allowing the pictures to speak for themselves. When the king awakes the next morning he discovers all about him representations of Lancelot's heroic deeds. To his dismay he finds among them a painting of Lancelot's meeting with Galeholt, the caption of which reveals to him Lancelot's feelings for the queen. This is the moment for which Morgan was waiting. She explains to her brother that Lancelot has loved the queen ever since the day he was knighted and that all his acts of bravery were dedicated to her (52:33-38). Not daring to tell the queen of his love, Lancelot languished a long time, until he met Galeholt who spoke for him to Guinevere. Their love then was sealed with a kiss. Morgan recalls to Arthur many previous episodes narrated hundreds of pages earlier.[25] The theme of Lancelot's love for Guinevere extends far back into the past, connecting many episodes across long intervals and thus giving coherence to the different parts of the *Lancelot*.

The intrusion of the past at this point in the romance is significant in two ways. In the first place, it is essential to the unfolding of the plot. With Lancelot's absence from court an impasse had been reached. Only outside intervention could upset the king anew and maintain suspense. Secondly, the episodes develop and clarify the theme of love. Morgan's love for Lancelot causes her to become instrumental in the breaking up of the bond between Arthur and Lancelot. In this way the episodes reflect the theme of the destructive force of love. At the same time Morgan's words recall a past event of the greatest importance, which shows us Lancelot's love of Guinevere in a new light. By tracing it back to his investiture, she reminds us that Lancelot was knighted by the queen and not by the king. This explains why he considers himself her knight and why he owes her his first loyalty. As Rosemond Tuve remarks, "In the prose *Lancelot,* the sleights through which Lancelot obtains even his sword from Guinevere and is her knight, not the king's, symbolize a cleavage that is also symbolized by their adulterous relation; and moral explanations of the decline of the Round Table on grounds of their simple unchastity have the same over-simplicity as do modern complaints about the 'small' role of the court. . . ."[26] Tuve's observation offers us a perspective from which we see Lancelot's love for Guinevere going beyond a personal relationship between two individuals, becoming, rather, a symbol of Lancelot's divided loyalties. Since one cannot be devoted to two masters, peace with both the king and the queen is impossible for Lancelot. For reasons rooted in the past, his allegiance to the queen has precedence over his loyalty to the king. It follows that, when Guinevere finally accepts and responds to his devotion, a break with the king is unavoidable.

Lancelot is not the only one whose present misadventures have their origin in past conflicts. Gawain's behavior is continually viewed in the light of his misconduct during the quest of the Holy Grail. From the moment he enters the scene, he is presented to us as a sinner who has killed eighteen knights. Throughout the romance his past accompanies him—and, lest he or the reader forget—damsels appear twice to recall its shame. When, on Gawain's insistence, Arthur and Gawain assemble their armies to attack Lancelot in Gaunes, an old lady warns them that their enterprise is doomed. She reminds Gawain of what was announced to him at the Fisher King's, where he met with such shame and ugliness.[27] It thus appears to us that Gawain's *démesure* and his ruthless pursuit of the war against Lancelot are an extension of his behavior in the quest adventures, and that the eighteen knights "prefigure" the many dead who will fall in the wars resulting from his insistence on revenge.

Arthur also is visited by an old sin, in the person of Mordred. Mordred is first presented as one of the king's nephews. We are therefore surprised to hear toward the end of the romance, that he is actually Arthur's illegitimate son! When the king receives word of Mordred's treason, he cries out: "Ha! Mordred, or me fez tu connoistre que tu ies li serpenz que ge vi jadis eissir de mon ventre, qui ma terre ardoit et se prenoit a moi. Mes onques peres ne fist autretant de fill comme ge ferai de toi, car ge t'ocirrai a mes deus meins, ce sache touz li siecles, ne ja Dex ne vueille que tu muires d'autrui meins que des moies" (164:5-12). No further explanation is given here. It is assumed that the reader remembers the details from preceding romances.

In one of these,[28] Lancelot discovers from a letter that Mordred
is the fruit of an illegitimate relationship between Arthur and his
sister, the queen of Orcany. The story was first told much earlier
in the *Cycle*. In the *Estoire de Merlin* and the *Suite du Merlin* we
learn that Arthur did not realize that he was with his sister.[29]
In possession of this information, we see him as the victim of
circumstances rather than as guilty of incest, and his "crime"
as *mescheance* rather than sin. It is then his natural son who
betrays Arthur's confidence and thereby causes the final ruin of
a realm already weakened by internal division. Mordred leads
Arthur's former knights and vassals in the attack on his father.
Arthur's wish to avenge himself by killing Mordred with his own
hands will be fulfilled. When many of the great knights lie dead
on the battlefield, father and son still remain, locked in mortal
combat. Arthur kills Mordred, but is himself mortally wounded
by him. In this tragic turn of events we clearly see the hand of
fate. Arthur has begotten a son who causes his father's death
and the destruction of the realm. In the words of Eugène Vinaver: "victime du destin, il en devient en même temps le com-
plice."[30]

Through an action in the past, Morgan le Fay indirectly
causes her brother's death. In a preceding romance, Morgan,
in a fit of fury, had stolen the scabbard of Arthur's sword.
This scabbard possessed the magic power of making him invulnerable. Its loss deprives him of supernatural protection and
thus makes it possible for him to be mortally wounded at Salisbury Plain. In this manner Morgan's scheming joins the other
forces that have been at work to bring Arthur to his death.[31]

The past and the supernatural are thus interwoven with
present events, to provide a multiplicity of themes all leading
toward Arthur's downfall. The cohesive element in this diversity
of themes is the presence of fate, revealed through the interlace
pattern. From the outset it is made clear to the reader that
Arthur and his company are doomed. The series of interlaced
events shows that the outcome of the protagonists' adventures
is out of their control. We know therefore that disaster is inevitable. But we do not know when and how it will come to
pass. The two pendulum movements between suspicion and trust
on the part of Arthur and Guinevere leave the reader uncertain
as to where Lancelot's conflicting loyalties will lead him until

his final confrontation with the king. Interlace thus produces suspense as well as a sense of doom.[32]

THE FUTURE ANTICIPATED
through Repetition and Analogy

Not for a moment does the author let us—or his heroes—forget the final outcome of the adventures. The future catastrophe is constantly announced in the form of predictions, visions, warnings, presentiments, and prefigurations.

Predictions, visions, and warnings state explicitly the arrival of certain events in the future. Repetition with variation is used effectively here. This technique was one of the main devices used in the composition of the early medieval epic. Once again we have to refer to the *laisses similaires* mentioned earlier to illustrate the narrative device of juxtaposition. In this instance we are not interested in their paratactic structure, but in their repetitive nature. We are here closer to the first type of *laisses similaires,* according to Pope's distinction, in which a certain action or theme is described repeatedly. However, the theme is not always phrased in exactly the same manner. Small variations occur which give it a slightly different nuance or provide us gradually with more precise information.

In the present romance, repetition is often used to remind the heroes of their inevitable fate. Such is the case with the prediction of the terrible war to come. The phrase is first used by Lancelot's brother Hector (66) when he returns with Bohort from the tournament at Camelot. They wonder why Lancelot did not appear there. Bohort expresses fear that his lord is upset by the queen's anger. He curses the hour in which their love was born, and he says that he is afraid that much worse is still to come because of it. To which Hector adds: ". . .vos verroiz encore entre nostre parenté et le roi Artu la greigneur guerre que vos onques veissiez et tout por ceste chose." These menacing words about the outbreak of a war more terrible than any before are repeated several times by different heroes. They form a refrain which runs through the romance, ringing an ominous note. In Hector's words regarding the greatest of all wars, two elements can be distinguished. First, a link is established between this war and the love between Lancelot and Guinevere. Secondly, we are told that the war will be waged between King Arthur and the family of King Ban. Hector foresees that he and his relatives will become Arthur's enemies, for when it comes to an open conflict between Lancelot and the king, Hector and his family will naturally choose Lancelot's side.

Gawain expresses a similar foreboding, though more vaguely. When the king urges his nephews to tell him what they were talking about—Lancelot's love—Gawain refuses, for if the king knew, "il en porroit avenir tieus max que onques a vostre tens n'avint si grant" (85:69-70). Agravain, pretending reluctance at first, finally gives in to the king's insistence and betrays Lancelot's secret to him. The king, shaken, swears vengeance, but Guerrehet advises caution, for if Lancelot should die, "li parentez le roi Ban commencera la guerre contre vos si grant et si merveilleuse que li plus poissant de tout vostre reigne i avront assez a meintenir" (86:53-57). Although the war will come about in a different way from the one Guerrehet envisions here, he too realizes that the family of King Ban will become their enemy and he is concerned about the threat they pose to the safety of the realm. Guerrehet continues: "Et vous meïsmes, se Dex ne le fet, si en porroiz estre ocis, a ce qu'il baeront plus a Lancelot vengier que a eus garantir." Guerrehet is the first of the heroes to mention the possibility of Arthur's death as a result of family vengeance.

Shortly afterwards, the refrain is taken up again by Bohort. Lancelot, uneasy about his cool reception from the king, asks Bohort for what reason the king could be angry with him. Bohort suspects that rumors regarding Lancelot and the queen have reached Arthur and he warns Lancelot: "Ore esgardez que vous ferez, que nos somes venu a la guerre qui ja ne prendra fin" (89:8-9). Bohort adds here a new detail to the previous predictions: the war will not only be the worst that ever took place, but it will also be without end. A little later, he clarifies the meaning of this in an exchange with Lancelot, after the latter has been caught in the trap laid for him by Agravain. Bohort now sees his gloomy prediction close to its realization: "Or verroiz la guerre commencier qui jamés ne prendra fin a nos vivans" (90:87-88). The war will be without end for them, because all will meet their death before it is over.

When Lancelot hears that it was he who killed Gaheriet, the war becomes a certainty for him as well: "Or poons nos bien dire, fet Lancelos, que jamés n'avrons pes au roi Artu ne a monseigneur Gauvain por amour de Gaheriet, car or commencera la guerre qui jamés ne prendra fin" (96:14-15). While the last words repeat the refrain, the first part of Lancelot's statement differs considerably from previous predictions. Until now, the war was expected to settle a dispute between Lancelot and the king, caused by Lancelot's love for the queen. But with Gaheriet's death, the burden of initiating the war shifts to both the king and Gawain and the direct cause is no longer Lancelot's love, but his *mescheance* of unknowingly killing Gaheriet.

The effect of the repeated prediction of war is threefold. As a recurring theme, it lends an ominous tone to the first part of the romance, and therefore contributes as such to the downward movement, for it presents the war as inescapable. This provokes in the reader a feeling of anxious anticipation, and thus heightens the tension. At the same time, the slight variations on the theme give us a gradually more detailed picture of the coming catastrophe. The terrible war becomes the final war for the heroes, for all will be slain in it, perhaps even the king. Besides these slight variations, we have noticed a remarkable change in the refrain regarding the cause of war and those who will declare it. But, different as Lancelot's prediction is from the others, the situations expressed are analogous. In both, the family rallies to avenge dishonor brought upon one of its members. In Lancelot's case, it is assumed by all that the family of King Ban will become Arthur's enemy, either by siding with Lancelot in his conflict with the king, or, in the case of Lancelot's death, out of revenge. Questions about the justice of the cause of war or its possible consequences are irrelevant, for the obligation to defend the family honor is absolute. Gawain has therefore precisely the same duty to avenge Gaheriet's death as Lancelot's relatives would have to come to Lancelot's aid. Lancelot is fully aware of this. When he discovers that he has killed

Gaheriet, he sees immediately that war with the king and Gawain is now unavoidable. We should bear this in mind as we follow Gawain's relentless pursuit of his former friend. His sin consists in his *démesure*, his lack of "measure;" he carries revenge so far beyond the call of duty that it becomes an obsession blinding him to reason and sentiments other than hate. The analogous predictions have thus offered us the perspective in which to view Gawain's future conduct, for the repeated assumptions on both sides that war will break out because Lancelot's relatives will fight on his side against Arthur, served to prepare as well as justify Gawain's revenge for the death of his brother.

With the fulfillment of its prediction, the refrain of the war-to-come is suspended, to be taken up again later. In the second part of the romance announcements of the future catastrophe most often take the form of warnings, dreams, and visions. Warnings are sometimes given by damsels gifted with clairvoyance. They seem to be messengers from the other world who enter briefly into the adventures to predict, threaten, or scold the heroes, as the later, blinded by pride and revenge, hasten to their downfall.

A first instance occurs during the siege of Gaunes, when Lancelot sends a damsel to seek a truce with the king and Gawain. Their response, as we know, is negative. The damsel then addresses both in turn, warning and reproaching them. To the king she says: "—vos, qui estes uns des plus puissanz rois del monde et li plus renomez, vos en seroiz destruiz et menez a mort, ou li sage home par maintes fois sont deceü" (110:38-41). She predicts here Arthur's defeat and death, long foreseen by many wise men. Then she turns to Gawain and scolds him: "Et vos, messire Gauvain, qui deüssiez estre li plus sages, estes li plus fox de touz les autres, et assez plus que ge ne cuidoie; car vos pourchaciez vostre mort" (110:41-44). Gawain also will die, and through his own fault. She reminds him of the fight he saw at the Fisher King's palace between the serpent and the leopard. If Gawain at that time had taken to heart the hermit's interpretation of this fight, he could have prevented the war when this was still possible. She clearly holds Gawain responsible for the war, blaming his evil heart ("maus cuers") as well as his great *mescheance*. Both elements govern his conduct. He is indeed guilty, but at the same time pursued by *mescheance*. Sin and fate converge in Gawain's fanatic desire for revenge, the cause of the fatal war. Since the damsel is not of the heroes' world, her interpretation of Gawain's behavior carries authority and may be regarded as a guideline for our understanding.

A similar warning is given by an old lady who arrives, richly dressed, on a white horse, just as Arthur and Gawain prepare to attack Lancelot in Gaunes (131). She tells the king that he should not have listened to foolish advice and that he will reap no honor from this enterprise, for he will never take the city. Like the younger damsel, she condemns Gawain for having begun the war, and predicts that he will never again see the kingdom of Logres in good health. Her warning repeats and so reinforces much of the previous one, but it adds a new prediction regarding the battle of Gaunes: they will be unable to take the city, and Gawain will die from the effort. As the damsel had done before, the old lady refers to Gawain's stay with the Fisher King and tells him that the hour is at hand when the promise given to Gawain in that period of shame and ugliness will be fulfilled.

With the appearance of the two clairvoyant ladies, past and future enter into present. Gawain's actions are presented in the light of his former misconduct; they in turn point to inevitable death. On the one hand, then, Gawain could have prevented disaster if he had acted according to what was given him to understand at the Fisher King's palace. On the other hand, having failed to do this, he seems simply to be dragged along by a pre-established chain of events, set in motion by his visit to the Fisher King. We encounter here again the ambiguous position of the hero who is at the same time a sinner and a victim of destiny.

Before the battle of Salisbury takes place, Arthur receives a number of warnings, many in the form of visions. Twice Gawain had warned the king not to begin the war against Mordred. As he lay gravely wounded, Gawain expressed the hope that Lancelot, the best and most courteous knight of the world, would forgive him his evil conduct. He then urged the king to ask Lancelot's assistance in the coming battle. He felt certain that Lancelot would come, for he loved the king more than he, Arthur, thought. Arthur, however, refused, because he had treated Lancelot so unjustly (166). On his death-bed, Gawain makes a last effort to keep the king from final ruin. At the threshold of death, he appears to perceive more clearly what the future holds in store. He tells his uncle that if he is to die by the hand of any man it will be by Mordred's (172). After his death Gawain appears once more to the king. In a dream (176) Arthur sees his nephew, followed by a crowd of poor people who say that they have conquered the house of God for his nephew Gawain because of all the good he did for them, and that Arthur would be wise to do as Gawain did. Gawain then adds his voice to theirs, begging the king, in tears, not to assemble against Mordred, for he will either be killed or mortally wounded in that battle. The prediction of Arthur's death is expressed this time with certainty and precision. What was shown to be a possibility in Gawain's previous warning is now presented as an inescapable fact: Arthur will die if he insists on a confrontation with Mordred. The king, however, answers that he will have to take that risk, for not to defend his country against a traitor would be cowardice. Gawain repeats his earlier advice which is at least to send a message to Lancelot, for which Lancelot on Arthur's side, Mordred would not stand a chance. But again the king refuses, saying that he does not think Lancelot would come after what he, Arthur, had done to him. Repeated here are Arthur's admission of having wronged Lancelot, as well as Lancelot's unique valor, and Gawain's restored confidence in his old friend.

The following night Arthur has another dream which, though of a quite different nature, points to the same outcome of the projected war (176). In a vision Lady Fortuna appears to King Arthur. She takes him away from earth to a high mountain where she sets him on a wheel. It is the wheel of Fortune, and Arthur occupies its highest seat, from where he can see the whole world. This symbolizes the extent of his realm and the great power he has held. The lady then takes him out of his seat and throws him rudely down on earth, saying: "Mes tel sont li orgueil terrien qu'il n'i a nul si haut assiz qu'il ne le coveigne cheoir de la poesté del monde" (176:73-75). It is in the order of things that those in high positions eventually fall from their pedestals; worldly glory is transitory. The lady expressed this universal rule, which has no immediate connection with the preceding events. But she has chosen the moment of Arthur's fall so as to coincide with the other factors contributing to his ruin. In Lady Fortuna destiny makes a personal appearance to show the king that he cannot escape fate.

The next morning Arthur confesses to an archbishop to whom he relates the two visions he has had. The archbishop adds his voice of warning to the messages implied in the visions. He urges the king to turn back and ask for Lancelot's help. For if he goes to war now he will either be killed or mortally wounded, and a whole generation will suffer the consequences (177). The king will bring only shame upon himself. But Arthur's decision cannot be shaken. He swears by the soul of his father, Uterpendragon, that he will not return until he has fought Mordred. There appears to be no honorable way out of the situation in which Arthur is trapped. Although it has been foretold many times that only death and destruction can come of it, as king and leader of the fellowship of knights, Arthur must punish the traitor. And so, ironically, his obedience to the demands of chivalry leads ultimately to the dissolution of chivalric society. According to both Gawain and the archbishop, Lancelot's help could still avert the tragedy. But Arthur has a bad conscience. He cannot bring himself to ask help of one whom he has wronged. As a result of his support of Gawain's fanatic vengeance, Arthur's realm has crumbled, and he will have to face his mortal enemy without the assistance of his most valued knight. The consequences of Arthur's "sin" of having given priority to family loyalty over the welfare of the kingdom link here with those of his *mescheance* of having fathered an illegitimate son, in order to send him, as well as his knights, to their death.

The final and most definite announcement of Arthur's death is found by him in a rock on Salisbury Plain, where he reads the inscription: "En ceste plaingne doit estre la bataille mortel par quoi li roiaumes de Logres remeindra orfelins" (178: 19-21). The archbishop explains that these words were written by Merlin long ago. The fatal battle then was foreseen far in the past. The rock at Salisbury shows more plainly than any of the preceding incidents that it is destiny which decides man's success or failure, his life and his death. It raises the question whether the heroes could have done anything at all to change a course of events which was determined long ago. To what extent do their decisions matter if the outcome is beyond their control? Since the prediction must be fulfilled, Arthur, of course, does not change his mind. Neither, however, does he disclaim his responsibility: "se il m'en meschiet, ce sera par mon pechié et par mon outrage" (178:35-36).

On a few occasions the author speaks out himself to anticipate later happenings. Since his predictions are brief and appropriate to the moment, they do not cause any interruptions. They are, on the contrary, so well built into the story, that one is hardly aware that the author and not one of the heroes is speaking. When both parties prepare for battle, he points out that now the hour is at hand when the oft-repeated prediction will be fulfilled: "Einsint fu la guerre emprise qui puis torna au domage le roi Artu; et comment qu'il fussent au commencement au desus, il furent desconfit en la fin" (105:11-14). The author seems anxious to suppress any hopes which Arthur's initial success in the battle might raise. His intent here is not to create suspense, but to stress that the tragic outcome is unavoidable, in spite of the heroes' endeavors. His next warning appears to be motivated by a similar concern. Even though the queen is returned to the king and Lancelot has departed for Gaunes, Gawain insists on a continuation of the war. The king finally gives in and promises to cross the sea after Easter to destroy Lancelot's fortresses of Banoic and Gaunes, even if this should cost him his life (128). The author then hastens to add that the king will not be able to keep this promise. Again, he does not want us to be misled by Arthur's optimism.

In the following episode the king entrusts the queen and the kingdom to the care of Mordred. The queen foresees trouble, for she knows Mordred to be evil and disloyal. The author intensifies our anticipation by adding that it will be even worse than she thought. The king then demands that his subjects swear obedience to Mordred, on which occasion the author tells us: "et cil firent le serement dont li rois se repenti puis si doulereusement qu'il en dut estre vaincuz en champ en la plaigne de Salesbieres ou la bataille mortex fu, si come ceste estoire meïsmes le devisera apertement" (129:31-36). To the old refrain he adds a new detail, namely that the plain of Salisbury will be the scene of the final battle. He further relates the war to Arthur's misplaced confidence in Mordred, indicating thereby that their fateful blood relationship is one of the causes of Arthur's defeat. As the decisive battle is about to begin, the author picks up the refrain once more, again elaborating it (181). He tells us that not only the kingdom of Logres will be de-stroyed, but many others as well, because a great many knights will lose their lives. Deprived of its owners, the land will remain barren. The consequences of the war then extend far beyond Arthur's realm and include many other kingdoms as well. The author no longer refers to the death of Arthur as the end of the Round Table alone; he creates here the impression that with the battle of Salisbury a whole era will come to an end.

From the examples discussed above it would seem that the author raises his own voice first of all to suppress any unfounded hopes, stressing thereby that, in spite of the heroes' valor and their occasional success, they cannot escape their fate. At other times he increases the tension already present, or he gives us more precise information on future events, enabling us to see beyond the immediate context. He achieves these effects by imparting to us details which only he can provide, because they are as yet unknown to the heroes themselves.

Predictions and warnings in various forms serve, we have found, in particular to bring out the dominant role played by fate. But they also point out that each of the protagonists is to some extent responsible for the catastrophe. Bohort and Hector related the war to Lancelot's love affair. The two damsels accused Gawain of pursuing war and destruction. Finally the king is guilty of abandoning his realm to his illegitimate son. The mention of later factors does not cancel the earlier ones; the various references have equal validity and thus reveal the multiple motivation also brought out by the interlace pattern.

Announcements of future happenings do not have to be stated explicitly or shown in the form of dreams and visions. There is another kind of foreshadowing, which is intended to warn and guide the reader rather than the protagonists. It is not expressed in words, but results from a certain arrangement of the material. At some distance from each other, two or more similar events take place, which develop either along parallel or along contrasting lines. These are to be classified as examples of analogy rather than of repetition. The identical elements in the situations forge a link between them which exposes or clarifies a theme in a more subtle way than statements or visions could do.

Such a situation occurs, for instance, in the interlaced account of the three tournaments, followed by a combat, in the first half of the romance. The two combats in which Lancelot is victorious frame, as it were, the two tournaments he missed. The two fights he won were, however, not fought for the same cause. The first tournament was one of the many chivalric encounters in which the knights engage regularly in order to perfect their prowess. The fact that Lancelot went to it alone and not with the king and his company marks a first separation from court. During the period in which the two following tournaments take place his isolation continues but is no longer voluntary. We have already noted the role played by *mescheance* in this sequence of adventures, or rather non-adventures. Fate has decreed that Lancelot twice in a row be prevented from joining his comrades and pursuing his knightly duties. It is significant that Lancelot receives his second wound from one of Arthur's hunters, that is, by the hand of one who serves the king. When Lancelot finally rejoins the court and is once again the champion in combat, he fights not as before, in obedience to the principles of chivalry, but in the name of courtly love. Although Lancelot is, in fact, loyal to both the king and the queen, something has changed during the interval between his first and second victories. The two analogous events show that a shift of allegiance has taken place away from the king toward the queen.

In close connection with the tournaments are the two traps which the king permits Agravain to set for Lancelot. Both times an opportunity is arranged for Lancelot to be alone with the queen, while Agravain plays the role of spy, lying in wait to close the trap when the two are caught. Although this scheme fails the first time, the second time it is successful. Both times Lancelot and the queen are reunited after a long separation, and resume their *fole amour.* In the beginning, however, Lancelot is able to reconcile his love with his chivalric duty. When Arthur announces a tournament, Lancelot leaves the queen with her permission to join the knights in battle. The situation is not the same when Agravain sets his trap a second time. After the defense of her honor against Mador de la Porte, Lancelot draws even closer to Guinevere. He is now so dominated by his passion that he pays no heed to anyone else, and this is why Agravain's scheme succeeds this time. Lancelot's absence from the king, from his comrades, and from chivalric exploits, marked the beginning of an ever widening gap between Lancelot and the court. It now becomes clear that Lancelot cannot be equally devoted to king and queen, and Agravain's betrayal brings the ambivalent situation to open conflict. Lancelot is forced to choose. He elects to defend the honor of his lady against the king. No longer can he serve both masters; from now on he will, in the name of courtly love, oppose his lord and comrades.

The significance of the partial analogy between Bohort's accidental wounding of Lancelot and Lancelot's accidental killing of Gaheriet is not immediately clear. Perhaps the first accident serves to point out that man should not be blamed for the effects of *mescheance*. This is illustrated by Lancelot's reaction when Bohort confesses. When Bohort explains to his cousin that he had not recognized him and therefore should not be blamed, Lancelot laughingly forgives him. He promises never to bring the matter up again; he even praises Bohort and Hector for their prowess. The understanding and forgiveness shown here by Lancelot, the victim, should also apply when he is himself the perpetrator of a similar though more serious act.

At a great distance from each other we find two analogous episodes, each involving one of the two protagonists. Those who escort Gawain's body to its resting place at Camelot stop over at the castle of Beloé. When the lady of Beloé recognizes Gawain, she throws herself upon his body, crying out that Gawain was the only man she ever loved. She must pay for this confession with her life, for when her husband hears it he kills her in a fit of jealousy. In the chapter on divided loyalties we have seen that this episode shows Gawain's courtesy as a positive trait juxtaposed to his *outrage*. But the incident itself appears as an afterthought, perhaps inserted later in the text, rather than as an integral part of it, for the lady of Beloé has not been mentioned before. The episode is not prepared for in any way by previous adventures, nor in preceding romances. The lady of Beloé appears out of the blue, makes her statement, and then disappears from the scene.[1] We fail to see the relation of this episode to the rest of the narrative until we recall a similar occurrence which took place more than a hundred paragraphs earlier, namely in the Escalot sequence. The lady of Beloé loves Gawain in the same way as the maiden of Escalot loved Lancelot, with an exclusive love. Both die as a result of this love. The second episode becomes relevant when we relate it to the first, for both illustrate the destructive force of love, and behind it, the presence of *mescheance* claiming the lives of innocent victims. The similarity between the two incidents shows also that Gawain has more in common with Lancelot than bravery alone. To view him as the ruthless avenger as compared to Lancelot, the courtly lover, is too simple, for Gawain also is valued highly by the ladies, many of whom he protected or rescued. He does not lack the qualities of a courtly lover, but in him these do not prevail as in Lancelot, for they are subordinated to his loyalty to family and king. We can now say that by means of analogy the former episode prepares the latter: the incident of the lady of Beloé is seen to be an integral part of the narrative and assumes added significance.

Prefiguration is a form of analogy in which one event, which may at first seem gratuitous, serves to foreshadow a later similar occurrence. An example of this is the series of epitaphs—printed in our text in capital letters—which stand like signposts along the route which the heroes travel.[2] They point toward death, serving the protagonists and us as constant reminders of the fact that they are unable to escape their fate. The first epitaph is for the brother of Mador de la Porte. The inscription not only bears the name of the dead, it also mentions poison as the cause of death and accuses the queen of administering it: "ICI GIST GAHERIZ LI BLANS DE KARAHEU, LI FRERE MADOR DE LA PORTE, QUE LA REINE FIST MORIR PAR VENIM" (63:11-13). The death of Mador's brother is soon followed by that of the maiden of Escalot. Her epitaph reads: "ICI GIST LA DAMOISELE D'ESCALOT QUI POR L'AMOR DE LANCELOT MORUT" (73:8-9). The wording on this tombstone is milder than the previous one, for though it relates the maiden's death to Lancelot, it does not point an accusing finger at him. We have seen how these two epitaphs, when seen side by side, reveal the active role played by destiny in the adventures. They also serve as prefigurations, warning the reader that he may find other victims of fate along his path.

It is in fact not long before we come upon a third epitaph, that of Gaheriet, Gawain's brother. It states: "CI GIST GAHERIET, LI NIÉS LE ROI ARTU, QUE LANCELOS DEL LAC OCIST" (102:20-21). Gaheriet's tombstone marks the dividing line between the first and the second part of the romance.

Resulting from Lancelot's love for the queen, the death of Gaheriet is the incident which definitely splits the Round Table fellowship into two parties and triggers the war between them. Implicit again is the theme of *mescheance,* for like the two other deaths, Gaheriet's was the result of an accident. The epitaph, however, publicly indicts Lancelot.

After the outbreak of the war, many heroes die in battle. It is only towards the end, though, that we find another epitaph. It is that of Gawain, who has expressed the wish to be buried at Camelot beside his brother Gaheriet. He asks that the following inscription be engraved on their common stone: "CI GIST GAHERIET ET GAUVAINS QUE LANCELOS OCIST PAR L'OUTRAGE GAUVAIN" (172:29-30). In the hour of his death, Gawain repents of his fanatic revenge which turned his best friend into his enemy. The epitaph stands as a public confession of guilt, absolving Lancelot of any responsibility, and showing death to be the result of both sin and *mescheance:* Gawain admits his sin, but at the same time he mentions the fateful role played by Lancelot.

The next inscription we find is the one engraved by Merlin in the rock on Salisbury Plain: "EN CESTE PLAIGNGE DOIT ESTRE LA BATAILLE MORTEL PAR QUOI LI ROIAUMES DE LOGRES REMEINDRA ORFELINS" (178). Although this, of course, is not an epitaph, it announces a later one by predicting Arthur's death. When his time has come, King Arthur disappears mysteriously into the other world. As Girflet, the last surviving knight to remain with the king, watches from the shore of a lake, he sees a boat full of ladies approaching, among whom he recognizes Arthur's sister Morgan la Fee. They beckon Arthur to join them and the king rises quickly and goes aboard, taking his horse and armor with him. The boat then departs and vanishes as suddenly as it had arrived. Arthur is seen no more alive. His mysterious disappearance shows that he did not belong entirely to the world of chivalry in the same way as his knights: he was at the same time part of the enchanted world, represented here by Morgan and the other ladies. A mysterious hand emerges from the lake to receive Arthur's sword Excalibur. This passage recalls another hand which, at the end of the *Queste,* reached down from heaven to take the Grail and the Lance. The downward movement of Arthur's sword, instrument of chivalry, stands in significant contrast to the upward movement of the holy objects.

Girflet remains behind, alone and saddened by the king's departure. He stays a few days with a hermit and then sets out for the Black Chapel. To his great surprise he finds there before the altar two beautiful tombstones. One, however, is more splendid and richly decorated than the other. It reads: "CI GIST LI ROIS ARTUS QUI PAR SA VALEUR MIST EN SA SUBJEC-TION .XII. ROIAUMES" (194). The hermit tells Girflet that Arthur's body was brought there by some unknown ladies. Girflet thinks that they must have been those he saw in the boat with the king. Over the other tombstone he reads: "CI GIST LUGANS LI BOUTEILLIERS QUE LI ROIS ARTUS ESTEINST DESOUZ LUI." These words refer to a curious incident which took place after the battle of Salisbury. When this battle has come to an end with the death of Mordred, only Lucan and Girflet are left with the wounded king. They accompany him to the Black Chapel, where the king spends all night praying God to have mercy on his knights who fell in the war. The next morning Lucan comes in to see how the king is and to express his sympathy. When the king hears someone behind him he gets up, but with great difficulty because of the weight of the armor he is still wearing. He embraces Lucan, who is not wearing armor, so tightly that he squeezes the life out of him. He is so absorbed by his grief that he does not even realize what he has done until Girflet cries out: "Ha! sire, com vos avez mal fet qui Lucan avez mort!" (192:16-17). When Arthur sees that he has killed his knight with his own arms, he angrily accuses Fortuna. Rather than being a mother to him she has become his step-mother, because she makes him live what is left of his life in trouble and misery.

This strange accident which seems a little superfluous after the slaughter on the battlefield, nevertheless fulfills a specific function at this place in the narrative. As the last of a series of mishaps that have occurred throughout the adventures of Arthur's knights, it serves as a sort of punctuation and provides, along with the early incidents of the death of the maiden and Mador's brother, a framework for the whole of the romance. The king is no less subject to *mescheance* than were his knights. It seems that after being wounded by Mordred in the final battle,

Arthur's role is played out. Like Lancelot and Gawain before him, he has become an instrument in the hand of destiny in unknowingly killing someone he loved. His epitaph does not however mention any misadventures, but only the valor which enabled him to conquer twelve kingdoms. Posterity will remember him for his glorious reign alone.

The last epitaph to be erected is for Lancelot. Lancelot had returned to Logres to avenge the king's death after which he entered a hermitage. There he dies after many years of penance. He has requested to be buried at Joyous Guard in the same tomb where Galeholt, his companion in the early adventures, was laid to rest. Bohort and his companions inscribe over their grave: "CI GIST LI CORS GALEHOLT, LE SEGNOR DES LOIN-TAIGNES ILLES, ET AVEC LUI REPOSE LANCELOS DEL LAC QUI FU LI MEIUDRES CHEVALIERS QUI ONQUES ENTRAST EL ROIAUME DE LOGRES, FORS SEULEMENT GALAAD SON FILL" (203:14-19). This memorial bestows on Lancelot almost the highest praise a knight can receive. No mention is made of any weakness or failure. Only the place of burial, the castle of Joyous Guard where Lancelot lies beside Galeholt, brings to mind his love affair with the queen. For through Galeholt Lancelot first approached the queen, and it was in this castle that he and the queen took refuge and were subsequently besieged by Arthur and Gawain. Even though his tombstone makes no mention of it, his burial place thus bears witness to Lancelot's love for the queen and to the war which came in its wake.

When we now look back at the row of epitaphs, we notice that together they tell the whole story in a nutshell. They offer us all the essential elements: Arthur's glorious reign and downfall, Lancelot's great merit and misfortune, and Gawain's *outrage* and tragic death. They show the presence of sin as well as fate in the adventures. Their respective burial places indicate where their basic loyalties belong. Gawain is buried at Camelot, center of the chivalric society, where he lies next to his brother Gaheriet whose death he avenged so fanatically against his former fellow knights. Thus the site of his grave recalls his family loyalty in the same way as Joyous Guard reminds us of Lancelot's love for the queen.

Gawain's hostility toward Lancelot is prepared for in the first half of the romance by means of analogy and contrast. At the tournament of Winchester we see the king, who has recognized Lancelot in spite of his disguise, take pains to prevent a confrontation between Lancelot and his nephews Gawain and Gaheriet. He does not betray Lancelot's identity but he forbids his nephews to participate in the tournament, for he does not want them to fight Lancelot and possibly hurt him or be hurt by him. This, of course, is exactly what happens later when Lancelot, rescuing Guinevere from death at the stake, kills Gaheriet, and Gawain subsequently becomes his bitterest enemy. Ironically, Gaheriet would not have been there, had it not been for the king who commanded him under menace to guard the fire with Agravain. Gaheriet goes under protest, telling Agravain that he will never fight Lancelot. The analogy between the two situations shows that events which are destined to happen will occur sooner or later, in spite of man's precautions. The king has only succeeded in temporarily forestalling the unavoidable conflict and eventually becomes the involuntary accomplice of destiny.

The initial friendship between Gawain and Lancelot is mentioned many times and Gawain's behavior prior to Gaheriet's death bears witness to his love and respect for Lancelot. When he is trying to gain favor with the maiden of Escalot but finds that she loves Lancelot, he humbly withdraws in favor of his friend, saying: "Car il est mieudres chevaliers que ge ne sui et plus biax et plus avenanz et plus preudom" (27:26-28). Later, when all wonder why Lancelot was not present at the tournament of Tanebourc, Gawain and Gaheriet leave court in search of Lancelot. Their great attachment to Lancelot prepares by means of contrast the tragic death of Gaheriet at the hands of this very same friend, and at the same time it accentuates the complete future change in Gawain's attitude toward Lancelot.

When Lancelot has returned to court and openly shows his love for the queen, Gawain, assisted by his brothers Gaheriet ad Guerrehet, tries to stop Agravain from informing the king. But Arthur, his curiosity piqued, is determined to get to the bottom of this matter. He commands them by the oath they swore to him as vassals to tell him the truth. Gawain still refuses. He would rather be dispossessed and exiled than divulge

something which, he foresees, will cause greater harm than anything has ever done before. Even when the king threatens to
kill them, Gawain and Gaheriet persist in their refusal and leave
the room. Though the king calls them back several times, they
do not return. The brothers express to each other deep concern
about the terrible consequences if the king discovers that Lancelot has dishonored him with the queen. The court will be de-
stroyed and brought to shame, for Lancelot can call on the help
of all of Gaul and many other countries. Gawain and Gaheriet
clearly realize the full impact of the explosive situation. It is
their love for the fellowship and the kingdom as well as for
Lancelot which makes them do everything in their power to avert
the war, even to the extent of disobeying their lord and uncle,
King Arthur.

We recall this sharp exchange between uncle and nephews
after Lancelot's rescue of Guinevere. Gaheriet, who tried so
hard to prevent an open conflict, becomes one of its victims.
Because of his death, Gawain declares war against Lancelot, per-
petuating it in spite of Arthur's peace efforts. The situation is
completely reversed. Gawain, so anxious to avoid war, has
become its fiercest advocate, while the king, first bent on revenge, now takes over Gawain's former role of conciliator. The
analogy between the two situations shows not only the irony of
fate, but also the different kinds of honor in the name of which
each hero is willing to risk the peace of the realm and the future
of the Round Table fellowship.

Gawain was also close and loyal to the queen. When the
king condemns her to death, Agravain and Mordred immediately
agree that she has deserved it, but Gawain protests and refuses
to witness the death of her who honored him more than any
other lady. As he leaves court, he threatens to render his fief
to the king, if the latter permits such "desloiauté." Yet, while
Gawain is still closely bound to Lancelot and the queen, there are
already signs of a later change. As we noticed earlier, in the
Poisoned Apple episode Gawain is indirectly and unwittingly the
cause of the death of Mador's brother and consequently of the
accusation of the queen as his murderess. He is also, again without realizing it, responsible for the queen's anger and Lancelot's
banishment from court, because he reported incorrectly Lancelot's relationship to the maiden of Escalot. The fateful role

which Gawain plays in these episodes prefigures the suffering he inflicts later on both Lancelot and the queen.

Several of the episodes discussed seem at first obscure and gratuitous. It is often only in retrospect that we see them as meaningful and as integral to the narrative. We then notice that one such situation prepared a similar or contrasting one in the future, and that some incomprehensible mysterious events foreshadowed later happenings. Analogy, in particular in the form of prefiguration, serves to point out the omnipotence of fate and the impotence of the heroes.

MESCHEANCE, PECHIÉ, AND REDEMPTION

The two downward movements mentioned in Chapter I re-sult from the interplay of the various techniques of composition discussed in the preceding chapters. Of these, juxtaposition contributes most to the spiral movement of suspense by bring-ing out the divided loyalties which tear apart the chivalric soci-ety. It is of particular importance in the second half of the romance, where these various loyalties lead to open conflict. Interlace on the other hand plays its principal role in the first part of the narrative. To the extent to which it creates suspense and makes a multiplicity of motives appear responsible for the final catastrophe, it participates in the spiral movement. At the same time however, the interlace design reveals the presence of *mescheance* in most of the adventures, giving cohesion to the diverse themes and episodes. In this function, interlace helps create the downward vertical movement. Repetition and analo-gy also take part in both movements. They indicate that both *mescheance* and *pechié* play a role in the adventures and share the responsibility for the fatal outcome. The question now arises how these two movements, the vertical and the spiral, are related to each other. How is it possible to reconcile *mescheance* or fate, which points straight downward, with *pechié*, the spiral movement of human failure? If the heroes' behavior is governed by fate, can they still be regarded as in-dividuals who are responsible for their actions? To respond to these questions, we must examine the roles played by the various characters.

In this romance the heroes do not, in fact, impress us first of all by their individuality. Lancelot is often referred to as "li mieudres chevaliers del monde," "li plus preudom," "li meilleurs chevaliers del siecle," or "li mieudres chevaliers qui vive." But nowhere do we find a physical description; we would be entirely unable to draw his portrait. Not only do we miss physical characteristics, we hear nothing about Lancelot's desires, moods, or qualities other than those immediately related to his chivalry and love. The same can be said of Gawain, who, although the best knight after Lancelot, appears in this romance mostly as the stubborn avenger of family honor. Sometimes the two protagonists even assume the dimensions of supermen. For instance, when the author describes the single combat between these two best knights of Arthur's court, he relates how they continue fighting, even after both have suffered great loss of blood: "si n'i a celui d'aus deus qui n'ait tieus set plaies dont uns autres hom poist morir de la menor" (151:44-46). Lancelot is able to resist even Gawain's miraculously growing strength at noon. When this hour has passed and they still continue the fight, the author repeats that, had they been other knights, they would have succumbed long ago, but they possess such great courage and endurance ("il ont les cuers es ventres si granz") that they will not stop short of victory (156). Their advanced age also adds to this "greater than life" quality, for Lancelot is fifty-five and Gawain seventy-six, when this combat takes place!

When the duel finally comes to an end with Gawain's defeat, King Arthur addresses both knights in turn. He recommends Lancelot to God, as the best and most courteous knight he ever saw (157). To the seriously wounded Gawain he says: "Biax niés, vostre outrage vos a mort; si est domages, que jamés de vostre lignage n'istra ausi bons chevaliers com vos estes ne com vos avez esté" (159:12-14). Lancelot and Gawain are here, as in many other places, characterized by hyperboles which magnify their knightly qualities, while detailed and distinctive characteristics are not mentioned. Never is the bravery of either Lancelot or Gawain questioned. They are the two best knights in the world (158). Besides their prowess, Lancelot's courtesy and generosity are praised, and Gawain's charity. All are qualities of a good knight; together they constitute the ideal of chivalry.

While Lancelot and Gawain are comrades at the Round Table and loyal to the king, each has obligations which eventually turn these closest of friends into mortal enemies. Lancelot's love of Guinevere leads to the death of Gaheriet and his two brothers and that of many other knights, and Gawain's fanatic vindication of family honor results in his own death, as well as the death of the king and most of the knights of the Round Table. Lancelot's passion and lack of discretion as well as Gawain's *outrage* are called sins, but at the same time their positions and the consequences thereof are shown to be the work of fate. Time and time again, predictions, warnings, and visions, draw our attention to the fact that the whole course of events was destined to be what it is. Merlin had already foreseen the fatal outcome years ago.

Mescheance and sin cannot be reconciled if we regard Lancelot and Gawain first of all as individuals. In that case, we would be confronted with a problem similar to that of free will and predestination.[1] If, however, we see the protagonists as representatives of certain principles or conventions, a different interpretation is possible, and the two movements appear to be two aspects of the same downward trend.

In this perspective we regard Lancelot as the champion of courtly love. Devotion to the beloved is closely connected with and actually forms part of the code of chivalry. A knight should be courteous as well as brave. A knight of the Round Table constantly has to seek adventures to test his prowess and be prepared to come to the aid of the king whenever the latter calls upon him. At the same time, the code of courtly love demands that the lover attend to his lady's wishes, that he honor her by triumphs on the battlefield, and that he rescue her when she needs protection. These two loyalties can support each other. As Bohort makes clear in his speech on love, the certainty of being loved makes a better and braver knight. For his beloved he will try to excel and thus also reap honor for his lord. In many courtly romances conflict arises from a temporary upset of this relationship. But at the end, equilibrium is restored and both loyalties continue to coexist in a delicate balance. It is, however, easy to see that a situation in which both lord and lady require absolute obedience, will inevitably lead to conflict. In this romance the author has created such a situation. When the queen is led to the stake, Lancelot has to choose sides. In order to save his lady, he has to disobey the king's orders and fight his own comrades. The death of Gaheriet at his hand leads to a definite break between Lancelot and the king. The potential conflict between knighthood and courtly love is now forced into the open.

It is Lancelot's sin which brings matters to a head. But what precisely is the nature of his sin? Generally, it is assumed to be his adulterous love for Guinevere. Thus Frappier writes of "la déchéance subite de Lancelot, récidiveste de l'adultère."[2] There are however, several indications in the text which seem to at least partially absolve Lancelot. At the beginning of the romance stands Arthur's statement that the force of love is such that neither reason nor common sense can resist it. We have also remarked on his reluctance to pursue Lancelot (Chapter II). Finally we know that Lancelot was knighted not by King Arthur, but by the queen. Frappier himself gives the following comment on this crucial event: "Moreover, the king by an odd lapse of memory forgets to gird the new-made knight with a sword, and this significant office of supplying a sword falls to the queen [Sommer, IV, p. 137]. The attentive reader is presumably given to understand that Lancelot's obligation to Arthur is thus curtailed and complicated wih another loyalty—to Arthur's wife."[3]

But if Lancelot cannot be held entirely responsible for his love of Guinevere, in what precisely does his *pechié* consist? The clue to the answer is to be found in the words of the maiden of Escalot: "car vos savez bien que amors descouvertes ne pueent pas en grant pris monter" (28:20-22). The maiden expresses here a well-known precept of the code of courtly love, namely the need for secrecy. Lancelot's sin consists in the fact that he has violated this rule. By his *fol amors* he has endangered the reputation and the life of his lady as well as the peace of the Round Table fellowship. His sin is indiscretion, which can be regarded as a *démesure* of courtly love, parallel to Gawain's *démesure* of family loyalty.

Is there a development in the character of Lancelot in the sense of an essential shift in his loyalties? Frappier definitely sees an evolution from sinner to saint: "Au début de *La Mort Artu*, Lancelot vit de nouveau dans le péché; à la fin il est au bord de la sainteté. On peut dire qu'il remplit dans le roman tout l'intervalle entre les deux états."[4] The turning point in this evolution and the beginning of Lancelot's "ascension morale" is, according to Frappier, his return of Guinevere to the king (117-119). We should note, however, that the Pope does not address Lancelot, but the king. The Pope rebukes Arthur for exposing his wife to death, and even threatens to dispossess and excommunicate him if he does not take his wife back and hold her in peace and honor. The basis for the Pope's severity to Arthur is the fact that the queen was not "caught in the act." Clearly a point of law alone, for the circumstances were highly compromising and no one questioned her guilt before. Most significant is the fact that the Pope does not direct one word of blame to Lancelot. The Pope's intervention sheds a completely new light on Guinevere's trial, for now the guilt is shifted from Lancelot to the king.

The king then sends a bishop to the queen to request her return, with the promise that he will honor her as before and that the affair will never be mentioned again either by himself or by others at court. When Guinevere turns to Lancelot and his relatives for counsel, Lancelot advises her as follows: "Dame,. . .se vos en fesiez ce que mes cuers desirre, vos remeindriez; mes neporquant, por ce que ge vueill que cist aferes aut plus a vostre enneur que selonc mon desirier, vos en iroiz a vostre seigneur le Roi Artu" (118:23-28). It is the perfect response of a courtly lover. In it he expresses his lasting love, and at the same time he sacrifices his own happiness for the honor of his lady. By putting her honor first, Lancelot has conquered his former sin of *démesure*. Lancelot does not surrender Guinevere to make peace with the king; reconciliation with King Arthur does not even enter into their discussion. If we can speak of Lancelot's "moral ascension," it lies not in the fact that he gives up his love, but that he becomes a more perfect lover.

From this point onward in the narrative Lancelot acts with the greatest courtesy and generosity to both King Arthur and Gawain. But this does not represent a change in character, for Lancelot has always possessed these knightly virtues. No shift in loyalties takes place. His love for the queen will last forever, as symbolized by their exchange of rings. Lancelot spends the last years of his life in a hermitage. But he does not enter religious service until after he has been released from his bond to the queen. In the romance, this happens when he learns of Guinevere's death. The Appendix makes this more explicit.[5] There, after the battle of Salisbury, Lancelot happens to stop at the convent where Guinevere has taken refuge. He is surprised to see her in a nun's habit and offers her to be once again queen of the land. But Guinevere refuses, saying that they have done wrong and should both spend the rest of their lives in the service of their Lord. Lancelot then takes his leave, begging her pardon for his wrongs. Either way, we see that Lancelot's first loyalty is still to the queen. Lancelot then enters a hermitage where he lives four more years doing penance by fasting and prayer. At the moment of his death, the archbishop has a vision in which he sees a large company of angels who joyfully carry Lancelot's soul to heaven. Praising God, the bishop says: "Or sei ge veraiement que de l'ame de cestui fesoient ore li angre feste si grant com ge vi; or sei ge bien que penitance vaut seur toutes choses . . ." (202:34-37). Penance has effaced any sin of which Lancelot might be accused. He is accepted by God and escorted to his heavenly place with great honor. The bishop's vision calls to mind Arthur's vision after Gawain's death. Both heroes receive God's grace, but Lancelot's death is accompanied by the greater glory. No longer is any blame attached to Lancelot's name. His epitaph lauds him as the best knight of Logres, except for his son, Galahad. When King Arthur shortly before his death asks Girflet to throw his sword Excalibur in the lake, he mentions that only Lancelot would have been worthy to receive his sword. And it is Lancelot who avenges the king's death upon Mordred's sons—his is the final victory. It is clear that Lancelot emerges as the hero of the romance.

While Lancelot's guilt is minimized in the second part of the romance, that of Gawain is stressed. Lancelot is continually praised for his courtesy and generosity, but Gawain is repeatedly reproached for his *outrage,* and called responsible for the catastrophe. His ruthless *démesure* stands in stark contrast to his chivalric behavior in the first part of the romance. There, Gawain had no trouble reconciling family loyalty with his knighthood, in particular since King Arthur is both his lord and his uncle. Gawain was not a fanatic family man who neglected his fellow knights for his relatives. Quite the contrary. He and Lancelot were the closest of friends. We have seen that Gawain left court and even defied the king in the name of this friendship. But family honor demands revenge when a member is killed and shame is thereby brought upon all the family. It is the duty of the nearest relative to efface this shame. With the death of Gaheriet and two other brothers this task falls to Gawain. There is no room to weigh in the balance the importance of brothers and friends, family and fellowship. The demand is absolute. Gawain has to avenge his brothers, no matter what the consequences. Gawain's sin is his *outrage.*

After Lancelot's return of the queen, Gawain remains solely responsible for the continuation of the war. In single combat Lancelot triumphs over Gawain despite Gawain's growing strength at noon. Since combat decides over right and wrong, the outcome points to Lancelot's innocence and Gawain's guilt. Lancelot had killed Gaheriet *par mescheance,* since he did not recognize him. Therefore Gawain's continued persecution of Lancelot is unjust. It is true that Gawain dies repentant and is received in heaven, as Arthur sees in a vision. But his worldly reputation is stained, to which his epitaph bears witness. Gawain's relentless pursuit of the family honor illustrates that absolute obedience to the family demands is incompatible with the knight's loyalty to his lord.

Let us now consider whether any of the other characters acts as a responsible individual, or whether, like Lancelot and Gawain, they are all trapped in conflicts not of their own making.

As the center and source of the Round Table fellowship, King Arthur would appear to be invulnerable to malign or indifferent fate—at least initially. For in many ways he is presented as more than merely human.[6] He is seldom seen in action. Rather, he is a static presence symbolizing perfect knighthood, remote from the adventures that touch and test the others. An aura of enchantment surrounds him: Morgan le Fay is his sister, Merlin his protector; he departs mysteriously, dying yet not dying. These connections with the supernatural heighten his elusive, almost godlike quality.

And yet in action the great King Arthur seems curiously ineffective.[7] All his reproaches to Gawain, all his attempts to reconcile the opposing parties, fail to halt the war which ends in catastrophe. He even allows himself to be caught up in the conflict whose excesses he has denounced. Clearly, then, Arthur, no less than his knights, is the victim of divided loyalties. He supports his nephew Gawain against his better judgment and against the interest of his fellowship and realm. Like Gawain's, his sin is *démesure*.

As a consequence of his forced hostility toward Lancelot, he later dares not ask for Lancelot's help against Mordred, and so he renounces his only hope of saving the kingdom. He appears for the last time as the victorious ruler when, with his own hand, he slays the Roman emperor. The events which follow drive rapidly to his ruin and the collapse of the Round Table. Betrayed by Mordred, he sees it as his duty to defend his honor as king of the realm, no matter at what cost. Those knights who had survived the war against Lancelot fall in the battle of Salisbury Plain, and Arthur's own death finishes the chivalric society. The fact that he is killed by his own son, moreover, symbolizes the dissolution of family bonds as well. Thus Arthur's death is both tragic and ironic: his pursuit of the ideas of chivalry results in the destruction of the very society which embodies them.

Sin and *mescheance*, from which not even Arthur is exempt, shape also the lives of those characters who surround him—Queen Guinevere, Bohort, and Mordred—in a direct or indirect way. Although the queen figures in many episodes, she does not play an independent role. The fact that an epitaph is mentioned for each of the protagonists but not for Guinevere indicates that she is not of primary importance. She exists only as Lancelot's lady and as a function of the theme of love. Her jealousy which removes Lancelot from court and her need of him after the Poisoned Apple incident serve to test his faithfulness. Her defense against Mordred's attack shows, of course, her fidelity to Lancelot, but the episode brings out more particularly Lancelot's courteous behavior as opposed to Mordred's crude desire to possess the queen. She finally takes refuge in a nunnery out of concern for her own safety, and the fact that the author has not credited her with nobler motives for a religious calling—as is done in a later manuscript given by Frappier in the Appendix—shows that he was not particularly concerned about saving her soul. She has no personal role to play. Her adventures are important only in as far as they challenge and put to the test Lancelot's loyalty.

Similarly, Bohort's role is more functional than central. He has two main purposes. Since he is one of the three knights who have seen the Holy Grail and the only one who has returned from the city of Sarras, he forms the link between the quest adventures and those at the court of King Arthur. As one of the "elect" he often displays insights and wisdom which the others lack, especially in the interpretation of courtly love. He lectures Guinevere at length on it, showing how love can support knighthood. But as he pleads Lancelot's cause, Bohort the counselor makes way for Bohort the loyal cousin. He severely rebukes the queen for her lack of confidence in Lancelot. Later, when the queen cannot find anyone who will defend her against Mador de la Porte, Bohort makes her suffer cruelly by saying that this is what she deserves: it is her fault that Lancelot is far away from the court and perhaps even dead. Still later, however, he is more kindly disposed and promises to defend her if no other help arrives. Several times we find Bohort serving as Lancelot's substitute: he offers to fight Gawain in Lancelot's place, and after his cousin's death he takes his place in the hermitage. Bohort stands here for family loyalty and as such he is Gawain's counterpart. There are already in his behavior indications of the tension between loyalty to family and to chivalric society. We remember, for instance, how he brusquely refused the king's invitation to return to court, leaving instead in search of Lancelot. When Lancelot considers returning the queen to Arthur as the Pope had ordered, Bohort advises against it, because he feels sure that Lancelot will regret it. At such times Bohort appears to be overly zealous, for his loyalty to his cousin prevails over any other consideration. In this way Bohort's behavior prefigures the excesses to which family loyalty leads in the person of Gawain.

Mordred, on first impression, seems evil personified. He conspires against Lancelot, betrays his king and father, usurps the throne by means of forgery, covets the queen, tries to take her by force, and mortally wounds his father. Issue of the king's *mescheance,* this devilish creature has been biding his time. When the fellowship of knights is weakened by internal division and the king is forced to leave the realm, the favorable moment has arrived for him. In persuading the king's vassals, by means of bribery and deceit, to break the bond to their lord, Mordred strikes a blow at the very heart of chivalry. Yet even Mordred is not pictured entirely as a villain; the vassals elect him as their new king in part because they respect his prowess. This election has come to pass in the following way. In order to possess the queen, Mordred has sent a letter, supposed to be from King

Arthur, to his subjects. In it the king says that he is dying and makes known his last wishes. He asks his subjects to accept Mordred as their new king and to give him their queen in marriage. This deception has the desired effect. When the period of mourning is over, the barons assemble and decide to act upon Arthur's wishes. They do so for two reasons: ". . .l'une, por ce que li rois Artus les en avoit proiés; l'autre, por ce que il ne veoient entr'ex home qui si bien fust digne de tele enneur comme il estoit" (136:29-32). The author here is careful to point out that the traitor Mordred is highly regarded among the king's former vassals. They praise him as a brave knight: ". . .il est preudom et bons chevaliers et hardis durement" (139:26-27). Even the queen cannot deny this (104:7-8). Much later, at Salisbury, when Arthur and Mordred are locked in mortal combat, the author repeats that "Mordres estoit bons chevaliers et hardiz" (188:32-33). In fact, he had to be, for King Arthur could only be matched with a worthy opponent. But in spite of his bravery, Mordred represents the reverse of the three major allegiances. Although a knight of King Arthur, he betrays his lord; in the role of lover he is far from courteous; and although Arthur's son, he rebels against his father and finally kills him. Clearly, Mordred is a most willing instrument of fate in accomplishing the final disintegration of chivalric society, set in motion by conflicting loyalties and *mescheance.*

The characters thus act out their fateful roles because they are torn by conflicting loyalties. We can therefore say that the two movements, the vertical and the spiral, are in fact two aspects of the same downward trend. While the spiral represents human trial and error, the vertical line of fate points straight down, traversing on its way the heroes' struggling attempts to deal with an impossible situation and coinciding with their failures. Fate is always present, though often invisible. Once in a while it appears in the disguise of mishaps and coincidences. At other times it shows itself openly, in visions and apparitions from the other world. Here lies the role of the *merveilleux.* In the *merveilleux* destiny takes on tangible, often personal shape. It interferes with the course of the adventures in the persons of Morgan le Fay, the two damsels, Lady Fortuna, and from afar, of Merlin. An aura of mystery also surrounds the arrival of the boat with the maiden's body and the return of Arthur's sword to the enchanted lake. Far from being gratuitous, these other-worldly characters play an essential role in the story, for they reveal to us the presence of a supernatural force. All these manifestations of destiny form part of the vertical movement. We can now see how sin and *mescheance* can be reconciled. If we regard *pechié* as the magnification of a weakness of chivalric society rather than as a failure of the individual, we understand that even the heroes' bravest efforts are doomed to fail. King Arthur's fellowship is not based on solid ground, but on a web of insoluble tensions. Its *mescheance* consists in the very fact that chivalric society embraces other loyalties than those to the king alone which undermine its unity. This is why the Round Table fellowship cannot endure.

Mescheance does not, however, have the very last word. One would expect the romance to end with the death of King Arthur, but this is not the case. Ten more paragraphs follow, describing how Lancelot and his relatives avenge the king on Mordred's sons, and how each of these heroes meets his death (195-204). We must not forget that *La Mort le Roi Artu* is part of the prose *Lancelot,* in which Lancelot is the central figure. Whereas Arthur's death provides a fitting end for this particular romance, the *Cycle* must properly close with the final adventures of Lancelot.

Left alone after the king's departure, Girflet becomes a hermit in the Black Chapel where Arthur and Lucan are buried. He serves here only a short time, for he dies eighteen days later. Meanwhile the two sons of Mordred, who had remained in Logres, hear of the deaths of their father, of King Arthur, and of many other prominent knights. They ride out, taking possession of the land without any resistance, for the owners were slain in the battle of Salisbury Plain. When the queen hears rumors of their outlawry, she fears for her life. Mordred's sons may well kill her for having so long resisted their father's advances. She therefore enters the order of nuns with whom she had taken refuge when Mordred gave up his siege of the Tower of London to fight King Arthur. As before, no mention is made of any religious calling, or even of any desire to repent. The queen's concerns are entirely of a worldly order.

When Lancelot is informed of King Arthur's death, he immediately assembles his barons and crosses the sea to avenge the king. He and his relatives defeat Mordred's sons at Winchester. The two brothers are killed, and also the Count of Gorre, with whom Lancelot's party had an old account to settle. On Lancelot's side, however, the victory has claimed the life of his cousin Lyonel.

Saddened by the deaths of his lady and his cousin, Lancelot wanders all night in the forest. The next morning he comes upon a small hermitage, where he finds two priests kneeling before the altar. In one he recognizes the archbishop of Canterbury, in the other his cousin Bleobleeris. Pleased to have found old friends, Lancelot decides to stay with them and to enter the priesthood. Lancelot's brother Hector joins them a little later. After four years Hector dies and Lancelot does not long survive him. As he lies dying, the archbishop and Bleobleeris are outside, asleep under a tree. The bishop has a vision of a great company of angels who carry Lancelot's soul to heaven. When the two men go inside, they find indeed that Lancelot is dead. Bohort, who arrives from Gaunes just in time to bury his cousin, takes over Lancelot's place in the hermitage and lives out his life as the others have done, in penance and service to the lord.

These last ten paragraphs which describe the events following Arthur's death, add a new and essential dimension to the narrative. They indicate a third and final movement in an upward direction. This lifts the heroes out of the pit into which fate has drawn them, and elevates them to a spiritual greatness which transcends all earthly conflicts. Celestial glory replaces worldly honor.

Frappier interprets events in this romance in the light of the preceding *Queste* and the heroes' subsequent fall from Grace. But although the same characters figure in both romances, the perspective is completely different. In *La Queste* religion is the dominant theme and the heroes' conduct is judged by Christian standards. In *La Mort* however, religion is hardly mentioned. To be sure, prayers are offered up before and after battles, and God's forgiveness is asked before death. But these appear to be no more than conventional formulae and gestures generally accepted as part of chivalric life. Religious practices are observed only insofar as they have become part of the life of chivalric society. Explicit reference to God is made only at the beginning and at the end of the romance, but in the main body of the narrative religion does not play a determinative role. One receives the impression that after the failure of the Grail quest God has washed His hands of the fellowship of the Round Table. Since they refused to observe His commands, He has left them to their own devices. He has abandoned the heroes to their fate. Only after their miserable failure has clearly revealed the inadequacy of human conventions, is terrestrial chivalry replaced once again by celestial chivalry. The fellowship of the Round Table, based on knightly virtues, has crumbled and gives way to a fellowship in Christ, based on faith.

VI

UNITY AND DUALISM
as features of Composition

As the preceding analysis has shown, the romance presents the double aspect of duality and unity. The two loyalties as represented in the two protagonists constitute the divisive forces, while *mescheance* and the upward movement are unifying themes. Both duality and unity are reflected in the form of the romance.

The dual structure presents itself first of all in the two parts which make up the narrative. We could draw an imaginary division line between paragraphs ninety-seven and ninety-eight— that is just after Gaheriet's death, for in this event two major movements occur: the adventures of Lancelot and the queen culminate, and the wars which lead to destruction are originated. We then see two parts of almost equal length, the first showing the destructive force of love in the person of Lancelot, the second the undercutting power of family allegiance as represented by Gawain. The tension in personal relations in the first half is reflected on a much larger scale in the second part, where whole families and even nations are in conflict.

A number of parallel situations link the two parts and stress at the same time the dual character of the romance. Both parts begin with a decrease in numbers of the knights of the Round Table, as a consequence of preceding events. Thirty-two knights fell in the quest of the Holy Grail, many of them by Gawain's hand; about sixty-eight[1] were slain in Lancelot's rescue of the queen. Although the two heroes are blamed for this loss of lives, *mescheance* is shown to be basically responsible. Thus both series of adventures begin under a cloud.

Three major zig-zag movements can be distinguished in each

part (Figure 1). Suspense results from the fluctuating relationship between King Arthur and Lancelot in the first half and between their families in the second half. In both parts, outside intervention resolves an impasse: Morgan and the Pope respectively make the action rebound through their authoritative interference in the adventures.

Just as King Arthur receives repeated warnings of Lancelot's disloyalty during the early adventures, he later has several visions and forewarnings concerning the outcome of the war pursued by Gawain. While Lancelot is doomed to inactivity during the greater part of his absence from court, Gawain is on the losing side of the war. During these periods of, respectively, isolation and misadventure, each has one chance to show his valor again. Fighting in the name of courtly love to defend his lady, Lancelot defeats Mador de la Porte, and fighting for his lord, Gawain distinguishes himself in the war against the Romans.

We have already commented on the resemblance between the love of the maiden of Escalot for Lancelot and that of the lady of Beloé for Gawain. The latter, however, is but a faint echo of the first both in significance and in the space it occupies in the text. But all these parallels show how the two major themes are reflected in the bipartite composition of the romance.

While the two parts thus underline the dual strain that traverses the narrative, the symmetrical composition of the romance in its entirety corresponds to the unifying themes of *mescheance* and faith. When we regard the romance as a whole rather than as two segments, we notice that the beginning and the end have several elements in common, offering us a well-rounded composition. The scene of the first tournament, Winchester, is also the location where the final battle takes place. Thus it represents both the first and the last victory of Lancelot, the hero of the romance.

Mescheance was first revealed to us in the opening paragraphs in Gawain's killing of eighteen knights on the Grail quest and, following that, in the Escalot episodes. It makes a final appearance with Arthur's deadly embrace of Lucan. Together these episodes provide the framework for the narrative. The fact that they are placed at the beginning and toward the end of the romance—not to mention the numerous other instances in which destiny reveals its presence during the adventures—indicates that *mescheance* is the perspective in which the adventures should be viewed.

As we have noticed before, however, not *mescheance,* but faith has the last word in the life of the heroes. Accordingly, the episodes of misfortune are in their turn respectively preceded and followed by references to religion. The mention of the quest in the beginning and the story of redemption in the final paragraphs form, as it were, a pair of parentheses, embracing the whole of the narrative and carrying it upward into a new dimension.

Bohort is the first to arrive and the last to leave the scene: he enters to report on the quest adventures, and at the end he appears just in time to be present at Lancelot's funeral. As the only knight who saw the Grail and then returned to King Arthur's court, he forms the link between the sphere of human conventions with their inherent tensions and that of faith in God.

The symmetric composition of the romance as a whole thus presents a unity which embraces the divisive structural elements. This formal aspect corresponds to the final thrust of the narrative in which religion triumphs over human ideals. Worringer interprets the gothic tendency to the infinite as an effort to transcend the tension between inner and outer world.[2] Similarly, the upward spiritual movement in the narrative represents the desire on the part of the knights to surpass the unresolvable tensions inherent in knighthood. In their reconciliation with God they find a peace which was destined to escape them at King Arthur's Round Table.

FOOTNOTES

Introduction

[1]Oskar H. Sommer, ed., *The Vulgate Version of the Arthurian Romances,* 7 vols. and an Index (Washington, 1908-1916). Vol. 6: "Les Aventures ou la queste del Saint Graal, La Mort le Roi Artus" (1913).

[2]J. Douglas Bruce, ed., *Mort Artu: An old French Prose Romance of the XIIIth Century being the last Division of "Lancelot du Lac"* (Halle, 1910).

[3]Jean Frappier, ed., *La Mort le Roi Artu: Roman du XIIIe siècle* (Paris, 1936). Later editions of this work, but without manuscript variations, appeared in the series "Textes Littéraires Français," 3me éd. (Geneva, 1964). English translations of Frappier's edition are:

The Death of King Arthur, trans. with an Introduction by James Cable (Middlesex, 1971).

From Camelot to Joyous Guard: The Old French "La Mort le Roi Artu," trans. J. Neale Carman; ed. with an Introduction by Norris J. Lacy (Lawrence, 1974).

[4]Ferdinand Lot, *Etude sur le Lancelot en prose* (Paris, 1918).

[5]James D. Bruce, *The Evolution of Arthurian Romance from the Beginnings down to the Year 1300,* Hesperia Hefte 8 & 9, 1, 2nd ed. (Göttingen, 1928), ch. 3 "The Vulgate Cycle."

[6]*Ibid.,* p. 431.

[7]Among these are: from a philosophical perspective: Alfred Adler, "Problems of Aesthetic versus Historical Criticism in *La Mort le Roi Artu,*" *Publications of the Modern Language Association of America* 64 (1950): 930-43; from a structuralist perspective: H. Blake, "Etude sur les structures narratives dans *La Mort Artu,*" *Revue Belge de Philologie et d'Histoire* 50 (1972): 733-43; from a historical perspective: R. Howard Bloch, "From Grail Quest to Inquest: The Death of King Arthur and the Birth of France," *Modern Language Review* 69 (1974): 40-55, and "The Death of King

Arthur and the Waning of the Feudal Age," *Orbis Litterarum* 29 (1974): 291-305; from the perspective of the concept of time: Paul Imbs, "La Journeé dans la *Queste del Saint Graal* et *La Mort le Roi Artu*," *Mélanges de philologie romane et de littérature médiévale offerts à Ernest Hoepffner* (Paris, 1949), pp. 279-93; from a social perspective: Jean Larmat, "Les Ideés morales dans *La Mort le Roi Artu*," *Annales de la Faculté des Lettres et Sciences Humaines de Nice*, no. 2 (1967): 49-60; from a psychological-realistic perspective: Peter Noble, "The Role of Mythology in *La Mort le Roi Artu*," *Studi Francesi* 45 (1971): 480-83, and "Some Problems in *La Mort le Roi Artu*," *Modern Language Review* 65 (1970), 3: 519-22; from a linguistic perspective: Jean Rychner, "L'Attaque de phrase et sujet nominal + Incidente + verbe dans la *Mort Artu*," *Revue de Linguistique Romane* 34 (1970): 26-38, and his book: *Formes et Structures de la prose médiévale: l'articulation des phrases narratives dans la "Mort Artu"* (Geneva, 1968).

[8]Marjorie B. Fox, *La Mort le Roi Artus: Etude sur les manuscrits, les sources et la composition de l'oeuvre* (Paris, 1938).

[9]Jean Frappier, *Etude sur "La Mort le Roi Artu": Roman du XIIIe siècle, dernière partie du "Lancelot en prose,"* 3me éd. (Geneva, 1972). See also Jean Frappier, "The Vulgate Cycle," in *Arthurian Literature in the Middle Ages: A Collaborative History*, ed. Roger S. Loomis (Oxford, 1959), pp. 295-319.

[10]Albert Pauphilet, *Le Legs du Moyen-Age* (Melun, 1950). App. 2, "Sur la composition du Lancelot-Graal," pp. 212-17. Also "Compte rendu de l'Etude sur le *Lancelot en prose* de F. Lot," *Romania* 45 (1918-19): 514-34.

[11]Frappier, *La Mort le Roi Artu*, p. xiv.

[12]Frappier, *Etude*, pp. 275-76.

[13]*Ibid.*, p. 228.

[14]*Ibid.*, p. 235.

[15]*Ibid.*, p. 243.

[16]*Ibid.*, p. 256.

Chapter I

[1]Throughout the text, the numbers in parentheses refer to respectively paragraphs and lines in Frappier's edition of *La Mort le Roi Artu.*

[2]Godefroy, *Dictionnaire de l'Ancien Français,* gives as the meaning of "mescheance": malheur, infortune, fâcheux accident; souffrance, misère; but also: méchanceté, action coupable, mauvaise conduite. Tobler-Lommatzsch, *Altfranzösisches Wörterbuch,* in the same way gives: Missgeschick, Unglück, and then: Schlechtigkeit, Bosheit. On the other hand, Tobler-Lommatzsch gives as the meaning of "pechié": Sunde, Unrecht, Schuld; but also: Unglück, Missgeschick. And Wartburg, *Französisches etymologisches Wörterbuch* says of "Pechiet": transgression de la loi divine. Action mauvaise. Sekundäre Bedeutung Afr. und Mfr.: malheur, infortune qu'on subit.

[3]Definitions are taken from William Flint Thrall and Addison Hibbard, *A Handbook to Literature,* rev. C. Hugh Holman, 3rd ed. (Indianapolis, 1975).

Chapter II

[1]In the visual arts, precisely the opposite takes place when successive events are shown simultaneously. Superposition replaces juxtaposition, for instance in paintings which depict Jesus' death, the women at the empty tomb, and the resurrection, one above the other.

[2]Erich Auerbach, *Mimesis: The Representation of Reality in Western Literature,* trans. Willard R. Trash, 2nd. ed. (Princeton, 1968), p. 105.

[3]Mildred K. Pope, "Four *Chansons de geste:* A Study in Old French Versification," *Modern Language Review* 10 (1915) 314.

[4]Eugène Vinaver, *A La Recherche d'une poétique médiévale* (Paris, 1970), p. 69.

[5]Frappier, *La Mort le Roi Artu,* p. xxvii. Alfred Adler, "Problems . . . ." (see footnote 7 of Introduction) sees in the juxtaposition of "good" and "bad" an expression of Aristotelianism.

Chapter III

[1]John Leyerle, "The Interlace Structure of Beowulf," *University of Toronto Quarterly* 38 (1967-8): 1-17.

[2]Henri Focillon, *The Life of Forms in Art (Vie des Formes)*. Trans. Charles Beecher Hogan and George Kubler (New York, 1948), pp. 4-5.

[3]Leyerle, 2.

[4]Eugène Vinaver, *The Rise of Romance* (New York, 1971), p. 77.

[5]Wilhelm Worringer, *Form in Gothic,* trans. and ed. with an introduction by Sir Herbert Read (New York, 1927).

[6]Vivaver, *The Rise of Romance,* pp. 78-81.

[7]Focillon: "Form becomes a rinceau, a double-headed eagle, a mermaid, a duel of warriors. It duplicates, coils back upon, and devours its own shape. . .", p. 6.

[8]The word "text," like "texture" and "textile" is derived from the Latin verb "texere," meaning "to weave."

[9]Worringer, p. 79.

[10]Vinaver, *The Rise of Romance,* p. 77.

[11]Ferdinand Lot, *Etude sur le Lancelot en prose,* ch. 3.

[12]*Ibid.,* p. 17.

[13]Henri Hauvette, *L'Arioste et la poésie chevaleresque à Ferrare au début du xvi siècle* (Paris, 1927).

[14]*Ibid.,* p. 277.

[15]Rosemond Tuve, *Allegorical Imagery* (Princeton, 1966), ch. 5, "Romances."

[16]*Ibid.,* p. 363.

[17]*Ibid.*, p. 226.

[18]Vinaver, *The Rise of Romance*, p. 76.

[19]*Ibid.*, p. 75. Geoffroi de Vinsauf (*Poetria Nova*, 5, 527, and *Documentum*, 2, 17) as quoted in Edmond Faral, *Les Arts poétiques du XIIe et du XIIIe siècle* (Paris, 1923), distinguishes between two kinds of digression. The first goes into another part of the same subject; the other introduces another subject which anticipates later developments, but with the assurance that the thread of the narrative will eventually be taken up again.

[20]*Ibid.*, p. 76.

[21]I have counted as episodes those scenes in which the maiden of Escalot is physically present. Mere references to her are not included.

[22]Tuve, p. 363.

[23]Richard A. Wertime also mentions Gawain's role in these episodes in his article "The Theme and Structure of the Stanzaic Morte Arthur," *Publications of the Modern Language Association of America* 87 (1972): 1075-82.

[24]Lot, in his chapter on interlace, traces a number of themes through the whole *Cycle*.

[25]Sommer edition of the *Vulgate Cycle*, 5.

[26]Tuve, p. 348.

[27]Sommer, 4: 341-349.

[28]*Ibid.*, 5: 284-85.

[29]*Ibid.*, 2: 128-29 and 1: 147-48. These chronologically earlier episodes were added later to explain and elaborate the theme of Mordred's incestuous birth, first introduced by the author of *La Mort*.

[30]Eugène Vinaver, "La Fée Morgain et les Aventures de Bretagne," *Mélanges de Langue et de Littérature du Moyen Age et de la Renaissance offerts à Jean Frappier* (Geneva, 1970), 2, 1081.

[31]*Ibid.*, 1079.

[32]On the subject of interlace see also ch. IV of my dissertation, "Structure and Meaning in La Mort le Roi Artu," DA, XXXIV (1973-74), 6006A-6007A (Northwestern University) and more recently Norris J. Lacy, "Spatial Form in the *Mort Artu*," Symposium, 31, No. 4 (Winter 1977): 337-345.

Chapter IV

[1]Frappier deplores this incident as a digression from the dramatic chain of events (*Etude*, p. 362).

[2]On Arthurian epitaphs in general see: Regine Colliot, "Les Epitaphes Arthuriennes," *Bibliographical Bulletin of the International Arthurian Society* 25 (1973): 155-75.

Chapter V

[1]Roger Pensom addresses himself to this problem in "Rapports du symbole et de la narration dans *Yvain* et dans la *Mort Artu*," Romania 94 (1973): 398-406.

[2]Frappier, *Etude*, p. 229.

[3]Jean Frappier in *Arthurian Literature in the Middle Ages*, p. 298.

[4]Frappier, *Etude*, p. 243.

[5]This addition occurs in a single manuscript in the Vatican. It is called the *Palatinus Latinus 1967*, a fourteenth-century ms. of *Mort Artu*. See: J. Frappier, "Sur un remaniement de la *Mort Artu* dans un manuscrit du XIVe siècle: Le Palatinus Latinus 1967," *Romania* 57 (1931): 214-222.

[6]Rosemond Tuve in the chapter on romances in *Allegorical Imagery* says about Arthur's role: "The royal person who looks passive to our eyes (contrary to epic structure), most certainly acts, but does so through his fellowship as through an extended self" (p. 348). Arthur is the "combined figure for the dynasty, the all-inclusive virtue, the spouse-to-be of the personified realm, the royal house through whom divine power flowed into

country and people" (p. 350).

[7]"In Arthur's guilt and sorrow over lost powers or mysterious inadequacy. . .we recognize the more primitive conception of a loss of sovereignty or unexpected decline of power through causes that can not be countered in natural ways, by heroic virtue or meritorious valor" (*Ibid.*, p. 353). "Most powerful of all intermediaries, a King can keep a human society erect for a time. But the painful lack and taint show up at length in him too" (*Ibid.*, p. 355).

Chapter VI

[1]A total of seventy-two knights is replaced, but this number includes those who left with Lancelot.

[2]Worringer, *Form in Gothic,* ch. 10.

Holy Grail

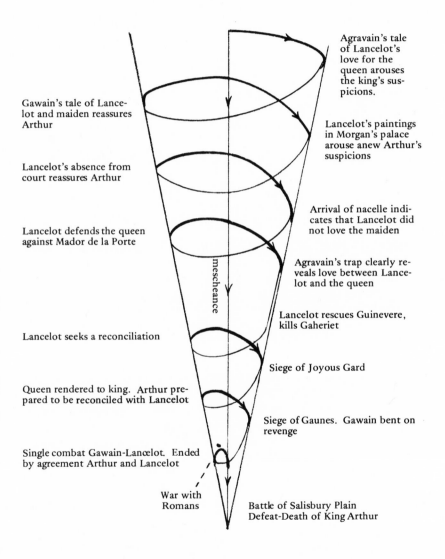

Agravain's tale
of Lancelot's
love for the
queen arouses
the king's sus-
picions.

Gawain's tale of Lance-
lot and maiden reassures
Arthur

Lancelot's paintings
in Morgan's palace
arouse anew Arthur's
suspicions

Lancelot's absence from
court reassures Arthur

Arrival of nacelle indi-
cates that Lancelot did
not love the maiden

Lancelot defends the queen
against Mador de la Porte

Agravain's trap clearly reveals love between Lance-
lot and the queen

mescheance

Lancelot rescues Guinevere,
kills Gaheriet

Lancelot seeks a reconciliation

Siege of Joyous Gard

Queen rendered to king. Arthur prepared to be reconciled with Lancelot

Siege of Gaunes. Gawain bent on
revenge

Single combat Gawain-Lancelot. Ended
by agreement Arthur and Lancelot

War with
Romans

Battle of Salisbury Plain
Defeat-Death of King Arthur

Figure 1.

Episode	Paragraph
Court	2
Escalot (1)	12
Tournament	15
Escalot (2)	25
Court	30
Escalot (3)	38
Tournament	40
Morgan's Palace	48
Escalot (4)	55
Court	58
Poisoned Apple (1)	62
Tournament	65
Poisoned Apple (2)	67
Escalot (5)	70
Poisoned Apple (3)	74
Court	82

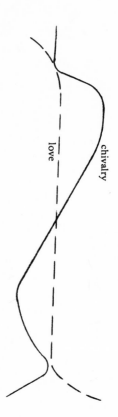

Figure 2.

Queen's
faith in
Lancelot

King's
faith in
Lancelot

+

Escalot   (1)

‾12.L. stays with vavasseur of Escalot.
   <u>Maiden requests that he wear her sleeve</u>
      at tournament
15.L. champion at Winchester. Unrecognized,
      <u>wounded by Bohort.</u> Gawain at Escalot.
23.Gawain reports to Arthur on L. and maiden-

Tournament

Escalot   (2)
Court

30.Arthur assured of Lancelot's fidelity,
      queen worried.
   Arrival of <u>Bohort who discovers he woun-</u>
   <u>ded his cousin Lancelot</u>
   Gawain's false report provokes queen's jealousy.
38.Bohort disbelieves it and leaves court

Escalot   (3)

   Maiden declares love to L. and hears he loves
      another; because of this she says
      <u>she is destined to die</u>

Tournament

40.L. absent because of wound received from
      Bohort
   Bohort c.s. refuse to rejoin the king,
      continue search for L.
44.Bohort c.s. find L. almost recovered

At aunt of
maiden
Morgan's
Palace

48.Bohort upset <u>that he wounded L.</u>
   Arthur, lost in wood, arrives at Morgan's
      palace

Escalot   (4)

55.Wall paintings shake his faith in L.
   Maiden approaches L. once more. Repeats
      she will die

Court

58.L. returns to court. Queen refuses to see
      him, L. leaves.
   L.'s departure reassures the king.

Poisoned Apple
      (1)

62.Queen gives poisoned apple to brother of
      Mador de la Porte, who dies upon biting
      in it. <u>Queen accused of murder</u>

(Forest)
Tournament

64.L. unable to attend tournament at Came-
      lot because of <u>wound received from</u>
      <u>king's hunter</u>

Poisoned Apple
      (2)

67.Mador arrives at court, demands satisfac-
      tion. Nobody offers to defend the
      queen.

Escalot   (5)

70.<u>Arrival of boat with maiden's body</u>
   Letter restores queen's faith in L.

Poisoned Apple
      (3)

74.Despair of queen. Punished by Bohort for
      lack of faith in L.
   L. appears and triumphs over Mador.
   Queen's honor saved.

Court

85.Lancelot and queen reconciled.
91.King's confidence in L. shaken—lovers caught.

+
Queen's
faith in
Lancelot

King's
faith in
Lancelot

_____ :   <u>mescheance</u>

Figure 3.